How Organizations Can Make the Most of Online Learning

How Organizations Can Make the Most of Online Learning

David Guralnick, PhD

BEP
BUSINESS EXPERT PRESS
Leader in applied, concise business books

How Organizations Can Make the Most of Online Learning

First published in 2022 by
Business Expert Press, LLC
222 East 46th Street, New York, NY 10017
www.businessexpertpress.com

ISBN-13: 978-1-63742-273-1 (paperback)
ISBN-13: 978-1-63742-274-8 (e-book)

Business Expert Press Collaborative Intelligence Collection

First edition: 2022

10 9 8 7 6 5 4 3 2 1

Description

In an age of accelerating business and technological change, the success of an organization depends significantly on its employees and how they can effectively learn and perform their roles. New technologies, combined with innovative approaches to the design of experiences for learning and performance, can help organizations boost their performance and improve their overall culture.

This concise book, written by an expert in e-learning and performance design, technology, education, and strategies, provides practical advice and insights for executives, learning designers and developers, subject matter experts, and others involved in organization learning, including:

- How e-learning is currently being used in organizations
- Research underpinnings of effective online learning
- How to create learning experiences that have a true impact on job performance
- How to create and support a learning culture in an organization
- Different types of online learning
- Organizational strategies for using e-learning
- How to build learning and experiences in-house
- How to work with outside vendors and consultants to develop custom courses, content, and learning experiences
- Online learning using different devices
- Best uses of artificial intelligence (AI), virtual reality (VR), augmented reality (AR), and other emerging technologies in learning and development
- E-learning management and administration (including learning management systems (LMSs), learning experience platforms, and learning analytics)
- How to maximize your online learning strategy
- And much more.

Keywords

e-learning; online learning; digital learning; learning experiences; online learning strategies; mobile learning; performance improvement; learning technology; learning design; learning experience design; user experience design; usability; learning analytics; content curation; collaborative learning; informal learning; workplace learning; corporate training; corporate learning & development; performance support; informal learning; workflow learning; situated learning; skills transfer; scenario-based learning; storytelling

Contents

Preface

Online learning, or e-learning, has become a significant part of any organization's learning and development strategy. But there's still a tremendous amount of unrealized potential when it comes to using technology to improve learning and performance. We're currently at a time of opportunity for forward-thinking organizations to re-envision their learning and development programs, in part by moving to different types of experiences that new technologies allow us to design, deliver, and deploy on a large scale.

My own background is at the intersection of education, cognitive science and user experience design, and computer science and artificial intelligence. I've spent a significant part of my career designing innovative learning experiences and consulting on e-learning design and strategy and have long advocated for organizations to move away from traditional read-and-test approaches to learning. Instead, I suggest new, creative, user-centered approaches to learning and performance that align with research findings in the fields of education and cognitive science—using technology, these approaches can reach a large-scale audience in a cost-effective way.

The goal of this book is to provide readers with a sense of the current world of organizational e-learning and also, perhaps more significantly, to explore the potential future. As new technologies evolve, we have more and more opportunities to reimagine and reinvent organizational learning, moving away from models that ask employees to memorize information and take recall tests, and to a world in which technology enables employee performance and is used to create learning experiences that feel relevant, meaningful, and useful to employees. In this potential future, learning is well integrated into employees' workflows and lives, employees have access to technology that makes it easier, more efficient, and more comfortable to perform their jobs, and employees' learning experiences focus on skills and performance and transfer clearly to their real-life work. As more jobs become automated, it becomes even more crucial for employee learning to focus on higher-level skills such as decision making and analysis. And in today's competitive environment, it's critical for organizations to provide learning experiences that will resonate with employees and make them feel valued and respected. The future of online learning can greatly improve workplace learning, performance, and culture, and opportunities abound.

Acknowledgments

This book would not have been possible without the contributions of so many people. Christy Levy, as always, has spent a tremendous amount of time talking through ideas with me and provided valuable comments on my drafts. Lara Ramsey provided invaluable support in getting everything together for this book. Many of the ideas in this book stemmed from conversations with others at Kaleidoscope Learning, including Veira Petersen, Boris Kontsevich, Anabel Bugallo, and Yidan Yan, and other colleagues including Hal Christensen of QuickCompetence, JC Kinnamon of the Practising Law Institute, Michael Auer of CTI Consulting, Antonella Poce of the University of Modena and Reggio Emilia, Christina Merl of Lab 21, Fernando Salvetti of eREAL, Patrick Blum of the inside Business Group, Alicia Sanchez of the Defense Acquisition University, Kinga Petrovai of The Art & Science of Learning podcast, Imogen Casebourne of the DEFI Innovation Lab, Sally Ann Moore of Learning Technologies France, and many others. I very much appreciate Ed Stone's work in helping me conceptualize this book and introducing me to Business Expert Press (BEP), and Scott Isenberg and Charlene Kronstedt of BEP for making this book happen. On the personal side, I could not possibly have finished writing this book without Irene Dominguez's support throughout the entire process. Finally, numerous discussions at conferences, including the conference that I founded and chair, The Learning Ideas Conference, as well as the ICL Conference (International Conference on Collaborative Learning, chaired by Michael Auer), Financial Services Learning & Development Innovations, Learning Technologies France (chaired by Sally Ann Moore), and others have all furthered my thinking and contributed tremendously to the thought in this book, and Jim Spoher's comments on a draft of the book manuscript were incredibly valuable.

CHAPTER 1

Introduction

Using Technology to Improve Performance

Introduction

The COVID-19 pandemic forced organizations to change the way they learned. While organizations already made substantial use of various types of online learning (or *e-learning*; the terms are often used interchangeably), suddenly they could no longer rely on in-person, classroom learning at all. Changes due to the pandemic helped organizations fully appreciate some of the benefits of online learning but also sparked discussions about how to better employ online learning methods going forward.

Computer-based learning, and later online learning, has been in use in a variety of forms, from remote live sessions to online courses to immersive simulations, since the 1980s. There have been successes in several areas, including learn-by-doing simulations in which the learner plays a role in a realistic experience and is able to learn in a "safe" environment—any incorrect decisions the learner makes in a simulation won't have a real impact on the company—and just-in-time performance support, in which training time is reduced in favor of tools that can help an employee work more effectively while on the job. Online learning has also seen a substantial set of "page-turning" courses, generally easy-to-produce courses in which the learner reads or watches information and then takes a quiz or exam. This method tends to be ineffective and not well received by its audiences. We'll get into the reasons for that later in this book.

Online learning has the potential to revolutionize workplace learning and performance, and we're at a time now in which, partly thanks to new technologies such as artificial intelligence (AI), virtual reality (VR), and augmented reality (AR), that potential could finally be fully realized. In order to take full advantage of new technologies and provide effective learning for modern learners, however, it's critical for organizations to take a step back and create or choose experiences that work for their audience to improve performance, rather than those that simply follow traditional educational methods using newer technologies. Technology is best used as a means to achieve certain goals, and in organizational learning, the goals are performance and behavior change.

A Focus on Performance

Corporate learning experiences often tend to be modeled on traditional education, whether in the classroom or online. Online learning regularly takes the form of courses in which employees read text or watch a video and then take a quiz in order to "check their knowledge." This type of learning experience is familiar and also simple and inexpensive to produce—yet it's rarely effective. There are a number of underlying reasons why other approaches are more effective, and we'll cover several of those in depth later in this book. However, at its core, the goal of workplace learning should be to improve performance—to help employees perform their best. The connection between being able to pass an information-based test and successful job performance is tenuous at best; along with other factors, good job performance in virtually any role involves the performance of skills, not the recitation or recognition of information. For example, consider someone who's starting an entry-level customer service job at a retail chain. It's not particularly difficult to take, and easily pass, an online course in which the test is information-based—for example, the learner may be asked to select which of several choices is a good principle of customer service. But being good at customer service involves much more than simply knowing the way that you're supposed to act—you need to understand how to use information in context, and also be able to put your knowledge into practice. Everyone knows that it's not considered good job performance to be rude to customers, but not everyone comes in with a great sense about what constitutes appropriate conduct and what doesn't. Learning experiences that focus on performance—such as a realistic, complex online learn-by-doing simulation with coaching guidance and feedback—can help people learn to perform, not just learn to recite information.

Different Types of Solutions

Recognizing that the overall goal is for employees to perform their jobs well—not to complete a course or even necessarily to know something but to be able to do things—allows us to consider and appreciate a variety of potential solutions, including, but not being limited to, educational experiences. There's a story in the Heath brothers' *Switch: How to Change Things When Change Is Hard* (Heath and Heath 2010) about consultants who, after a new timesheet system is rolled out, often fail to submit their hours. After training solutions fail, the company realizes that the issue is not a lack of training but that the new system is awkward and slow to use—the solution was to improve the system rather than to better train the employees. Process improvement, "just-in-time" performance support—providing something to help people perform their job just when they need it, the way a GPS-driven navigation system provides directions to a driver—and training/learning experiences all are potential ways to improve performance in both the short term and the long term. Within the world of learning experiences, there are numerous approaches; some problems may call for a simple, inexpensive approach, others for an in-depth, high-tech experience.

Using Technology to Create Learning Experiences

New technologies can help us reimagine and reinvent the way people learn and to greatly improve performance. Perhaps the key when it comes to employing new technologies in learning is to consider what types of experiences we want to create, and how we can best design an experience that makes use of the capabilities of a particular technology in order to do so, rather than simply trying to replicate common learning methods and experiences in a new format. Long ago, the apprenticeship model was the most common form of education; people who wanted to learn to be, say, a blacksmith would learn to do so by apprenticing to a master blacksmith.

The apprentice might start with simple tasks such as cleaning equipment, then grow into more complex tasks and skills, all while receiving coaching guidance and feedback from an expert.

The apprenticeship model is practical and effective, but it doesn't scale up well. When society needed to teach and train masses of people, the apprenticeship model simply couldn't handle the load—there were not nearly enough experts to work with everyone. The classroom model that we often see today—with a teacher or lecturer in front of a class—can teach a large group, but it's not, and was never intended to be the most effective learning experience, just the one that was practical to implement.

However, technology-based experiences—particularly those that are learner-driven, such as, for example, learning to fly a plane via a flight simulator—do scale up! If we create a great learning experience that runs on a computer or mobile phone, it can be made accessible to millions of people, or more, for essentially the same cost as making it accessible by 10 people. The key is to avoid focusing only on reaching a large audience but to look to create great experiences, often those that follow different methods than traditional learning.

Focusing on Learning and Performance Rather Than on Teaching

Traditional education involves a class of students and a teacher, who leads the class. Under this model, the underlying thinking is that the teacher has knowledge and will impart this knowledge to the students, and then will test them on this knowledge. This is a very different model than the apprenticeship approach described above; its big advantage is that it scales up well—one teacher can handle a class of 100 students, or 300 students, or maybe even more, especially in an online, virtual-class format. However, both research (e.g., Brown, Collins, and Duguid 1989) and practical experience have shown that people learn better when asked to do things—perform tasks, make decisions, create something—and that particularly in a workplace setting, where the goals clearly revolve around performance and skills, a learning-by-doing approach is a much better way to go.

A related concept is the idea of focusing on learning and performance rather than on teaching. The teaching model may be what most people are accustomed to, and what they think of as "education" in any context, but modern times call for modern methods, and we have many other, better options than traditional teaching when it comes to employee learning and development. Active approaches to learning (see, e.g., Bonwell and Eison 1991; Freeman, Eddy, McDonough, Smith, Okoroafor, Jordt, and Wenderoth 2014; Ruiz-Primo, Briggs, Iverson, Talbot, and Shepard 2011), in which learners are involved in the learning process—as opposed to passive approaches, such as watching a lecture—can be personalized and relevant, engaging and applicable. Active learning experiences can also often be integrated into an employee's workflow, so employees can learn while performing their actual job and thus reduce the need for training experiences that pull them away from their work. In addition, active learning experiences tend to be more accepted by employees— they put the learner in control and are not only more efficient than traditional, passive methods but also are more respectful to the employee, not treating employees as if they're small children (though arguments can certainly be made that traditional teaching is not the best method for small children, either!).

New Technologies in Learning

Forward-thinking organizations are looking at how to best employ new technologies, such as virtual reality (VR), augmented reality (AR), and artificial intelligence (AI), in learning. Virtual reality provides immersive experiences in which a user wears a special headset and therefore feels truly surrounded by the digitized world that's displayed in the headset. VR headsets are becoming much less expensive and more easily available, providing new opportunities for organizations to improve their learning experiences. VR is ideal for learn-by-doing simulations, in which a learner practices a skill in a simulated environment—the experience feels realistic and therefore transfers well to real-life work, but any mistakes and experimentation don't have real-life consequences to the business—for example, a computer technician might practice certain repairs in a VR simulation, and if the technician accidentally fries a motherboard in the simulation, it's not a real computer so no customer will be upset, but the technician will learn from their mistakes.

Augmented reality (AR) enhances the real world via technology; for example, Google Maps includes a feature that can direct the user through a major airport, step by step, by superimposing instructions and detailed information over a live view of where the user is (Haselton 2021). Figure 1.1 shows an AR map example from an airport.

Figure 1.1 Augmented reality using mobile maps

Within organizational learning, AR can alleviate the need for training by providing employees with more just-in-time guidance. Following the Google Maps example, an AR app for an audience of retail stockroom workers could direct them to find a particular item on a shelf.

Artificial intelligence (AI) is becoming more and more widespread in its use in different areas, from smart appliances to self-driving cars and many others. In learning, AI has the potential to radically improve learning experiences. Many current applications of AI in learning focus on analytics, and in assessing the strengths and weaknesses of employees based on their performance in a training activity. This type of information can certainly be useful, though there's a risk in overly automating performance and skill evaluations, especially at this fairly early stage in the widespread use of this type of AI. It's likely that the large-scale impact of AI will be felt in the creation of learning experiences that are much more personalized: the system will get to know the employee's strengths and weaknesses as well as their interests—everything from what types of learning experiences they most enjoy to what content areas might resonate best with them when used in an analogy—and function more as a coach. This model has the potential to greatly improve employee performance as well as their appreciation for their organization.

Research Underpinnings of Effective Online Learning

The majority of online learning currently in use resembles traditional education, translated to an online medium: people read, listen to, or watch something, then take a test on their knowledge, typically focusing on their recall of key facts. Research from the area of cognitive science (e.g., Brown, Collins, and Duguid 1989; Greeno, Smith, and Moore 1993; Lave and Wenger 1991) tells us that this method is effective if the end goal is memorization, but not ideal when the goal is performance. It's at best arguable whether memorizing facts is a useful goal in schools—students would be better prepared for life and work if their educational experiences focused on critical thinking and decision making over memorization— and for workplace learning purposes, the goal is clearly performance.

The design of effective online learning integrates research from several areas in order to create experiences that help people perform and do so in ways that employees will emotionally connect with. Relevant research areas include:

- Cognitive science and education (much of this work is now also categorized as "learning sciences"): Relevant work covers methods by which people learn best, both individually and collaboratively, such as Allan Collins and John Seeley Brown's work on situated cognition (Brown, Collins, and Duguid 1989) and cognitive apprenticeships (Collins, Brown, and Newman 1989), Jean Lave and Etienne Wenger's work on situated learning and communities of practice (1991), and David Kolb's work on experiential learning (Kolb 1984); how people can learn in ways that will facilitate remembering (see, e.g., Casebourne 2015 for a writeup with additional research citations about spaced learning, an approach that facilitates remembering); and how people can best process information and experiences optimally (see Clark and Mayer 2011) without being overloaded (see Sweller 1988 and Sweller, Ayres, and Kalyuga 2011).

- User experience (UX): Work in UX is incredibly relevant to the design of online learning experiences and is sometimes overlooked in online learning. Research into software usability (including that of Jakob Nielsen, Don Norman, and their Nielsen Norman Group—see Nielsen 2000—and Jared Spool, as in Hoekman and Spool 2010), other human factors areas, and how people use technology are all especially relevant to online learning. Usability testing (see Rubin and Chisnell 2008), the process of asking end-users to use a product at various stages and provide feedback and be observed, is also a key part of a sound design process. This work can include everything from collecting user feedback early in the process to studying how people use a prototype or beta version of a course or other learning experience.

Organizational Strategies for Using Online Learning

Forward-thinking organizations have an opportunity to make online learning a core part of their organizational culture. Traditionally, learning management systems (LMSs) have been used to house e-learning courses and content, and employees use the LMS to access their training. Employee responses to LMSs are frequently less than positive; for example, a 2015 study by Sharon Vipond for *Learning Solutions* magazine concluded that, within organizations "overall levels of LMS satisfaction remained mediocre at best" (Vipond 2016), and current anecdotal experiences confirm that view; LMSs tend to be cumbersome and unfriendly to use, and are centered primarily around a model of courses and content, rather than having a focus on performance and user experience.

Modern learners expect modern learning experiences that feel more like the experiences they have with learning and technology outside of work—as one example, someone who's looking for help putting together a spinning bike they purchased can usually find a video online that demonstrates how to do so. Such an experience is quick, to the point, and involves showing how to do something rather than just talking about it. Overall, in order to make the best use of online learning, organizations would be well-served to redesign their uses of technology in learning and development to move away from traditional educational models and take advantage of new technologies, along with research-based learning methods, to create new models of online learning for their employees. We'll discuss potential strategies in more detail later in this book.

CHAPTER 2

Types of Online Learning

As the COVID-19 pandemic hit and forced workplaces and schools to suddenly go virtual, much of the discussion of online learning focused on live virtual classes over Zoom and similar platforms. Such events certainly have a role, particularly during a time when workforces are often partly remote even during non-pandemic times. But "asynchronous" forms of online learning—those in which the learners are not in a class at the same time, and typically not in a class at all but do work in a self-paced way—make up a substantial portion of organizational online learning experiences and, as we look to the future, are likely to play an even larger role due to their potential to cost-effectively provide high-quality learning on a large scale, as well as to new technologies.

Virtual Classes

Virtual classes typically resemble traditional in-person classes but are conducted remotely. Zoom has become the best-known platform for virtual classes as, due to the COVID-19 pandemic, remote classes became much more prevalent. Zoom meetings can work well (when used judiciously) for smaller groups and support "breakout rooms" in which the class group can be divided into subgroups who have their own private discussions—live via Zoom video—for some part of a session. Zoom also supports live text-based chat, poll questions in which it automatically tabulates and displays the results, and other features that are regularly being updated and improved. A version of Zoom called Zoom Webinar focuses more on presentation than discussion and is particularly useful for larger groups as well as webinar and conference events. Zoom is far from the only player in this space; others include Adobe Connect, WebEx, GoToMeeting (and its GoToTraining and GoToWebinar products), and BlueJeans, as well as Microsoft Teams, which has continued to expand its capabilities and is in wide use within large organizations. Many vendors in this space also provide hardware and software to be used in classrooms and improve the quality of remote access, for situations in which an instructor or speaker is in the office, but attendees participate remotely.

Virtual classes can take numerous forms, but whatever the size of the audience is, active learning experiences are worth considering. There's certainly a role for periodic lectures, particularly talks from notable experts (either in-house or external), but staying solely with a lecture format is usually not ideal. Discussions, breakout sessions with specific tasks (e.g., solving a problem as a group), and the overall encouragement of communication are often sound approaches.

Massive Open Online Courses (MOOCs)

The massive open online course (MOOC) model became popular in the early 2010s; the first MOOC to gain widespread popularity was "Introduction to Artificial Intelligence," taught by Stanford's Peter Norvig and Sebastian Thrun in 2011 to an audience of 160,000 students, 20,000 of whom completed the entire course (McGill University 2021). The MOOC model typically involves a mix of prerecorded lectures on video, some instructor interaction and class discussion, and potentially other activities. MOOCs first became known as a way to easily reach a large audience, and to be available to anyone around the world—early MOOCs were indeed both "massive" and "open," and MOOCs have had over 180 million participants according to ClassCentral.com (Shah 2020). One very popular MOOC, Barbara Oakley and Terrence Sejnowski's "Learning How to Learn," had reached 1.8 million users by 2017 (Schwartz 2017) and is still being used today. The MOOC model has received, over the years, a tremendous amount of hype (e.g., the 2012 article in the *New York Times* titled "The Year of the MOOC"; Pappano 2012), followed by more than a bit of a backlash (e.g., *Time* magazine's 2013 article "All Hail MOOCs! Just Don't Ask if They Actually Work"; Marcus 2013), as the model as originally conceived—typically a course that lasts for 10–15 weeks, along the lines of a college course—tends to be impersonal given its structure and large-scale audience. However, the MOOC model has been modified and repurposed for the creation of "corporate MOOCs," which tend to be both shorter in length and more focused on applied learning than many traditional MOOCs, with some success. A model integrating MOOC elements and inventive self-paced active learning approaches, dubbed an "interactive MOOC" or "iMOOC" (Guralnick 2014; Guralnick and Kinnamon 2016) has been successful but has not yet found wide usage.

Self-Paced Learning Experiences

A significant portion of all online learning experiences are self-paced experiences, and the expectation is that the use of self-paced experiences will continue to increase substantially in the future. In self-paced online learning, there is no class, no live session, no communication with other participants; the learner simply works when they want. Many self-paced online learning experiences are courses in some form, which means they do have a defined moment of completion; some also have a deadline, either internal to a company or based on professional development requirements. But by and large, the learner decides when to participate in the experience, when to stop and restart, and often even which type of device to use (e.g., a desktop computer, laptop computer, tablet, or mobile phone).

Forms of Self-Paced E-Learning

Self-paced learning comes in a variety of different forms, and new methods and experiences can always be (and should be!) invented. There's a constant tension within learning and development (L&D) teams between budget and the ideal experience. A higher-end learner experience is often too time-consuming or expensive to create (in part due to the lack of fully appropriate software tools on the market, which we will discuss in more detail in Chapter 3), and L&D teams often feel significant time and budget pressure. There also tends to be a prevailing view in many companies, particularly at higher levels, that the key to effective learning is simply "content." My perspective is that the learning experience is critical and that the return on investment (ROI) on e-learning courses designed around reading and quizzes is often very minimal.

Self-paced learning can be very effective, but many of the commonly used methods are not particularly effective. In the sections below, we'll take a look at a variety of forms of self-paced online learning, starting with simpler and less-effective (if typically less costly and time-consuming to create) forms and moving to more-substantial methods.

Read/Watch/Test

A substantial portion of existing e-learning courses within organizations is of a form that primarily involves the learner reading some text and watching videos, along with taking a quiz, often termed a "knowledge check." This model is simple and inexpensive to create; there are numerous off-the-shelf e-learning authoring tools—software that can be used to create courses without needing to be a software developer—that facilitate the fast and easy creation of courses in this model. This online model also is very reminiscent of the traditional classroom model, in which students read textbooks, listen to lectures, and take exams.

While still quite common, this method is typically not effective—research (e.g., Newell and Simon 1972; Singley and Anderson 1989) has shown that people learn to perform skills much better by actively performing tasks and making decisions, rather than memorizing information and taking a quiz about it. As with any method, there are stronger and weaker ways to design and implement it—for example, a quiz that presents people with realistic scenarios and asks them to choose a course of action is generally much better than one that asks them to match terms and definitions, since the scenario-based model tests people on skills that may apply well to their actual work tasks. Nonetheless, the read/watch/test model is far from ideal, but remains in popular use due to its familiarity to training developers and to its low cost and fast production time. Employees also may not find this type of course to be interesting or applicable, which can in turn affect their view of their role and their employer. It's generally wise to use this format judiciously and look to phase it out as more efficient ways to create better learning become more widely available.

Traditional E-Learning Activities and Assessments

The activity formats most commonly seen in online learning also resemble, at least conceptually, traditional classroom activities and assessments. These formats tend to be easy to create and are familiar to people but tend to usually be less than effective, again because they ask learners to memorize facts more than to perform skills. Standard assessment questions such as fact-based multiple-choice questions and matching questions fall into this category, as do online methods that are a step up from these such as drag-and-drop quizzes, in which a learner is asked to click on an object on the screen and drag it to the corresponding answer. The activity in this case is not a meaningful activity; this is simply a standard quiz question with a bit of physical activity added. As with the read/watch/test learning model described above, these methods are inexpensive and fast to implement but tend to not be particularly effective at accurately assessing employees' skills in ways that reflect or predict how they will perform on the job, and also tend not to make employees feel valued.

Learn-By-Doing Simulations

Simulation-based learning has been around for quite some time (see, for example, Guralnick 1996) in various forms. The earliest documented computer-based training simulation was the Boston Chicken Cashier Trainer program, created in 1991 (see Guralnick 1996; Freedman 1994), which taught cashiers at a fast-food chain how to ring up orders efficiently and accurately by asking them to watch a customer place an order via video and then actually ring up the order using a computer-based replica of the specialized cash register used at the restaurant. This learning-by-doing method was realistic and transferred to the actual job—learners weren't asked to memorize or study how to be a cashier, but to practice doing it in a "safe" environment—if they made mistakes in the training simulation, those mistakes wouldn't result in undercharging customers and losing money, overcharging customers and upsetting them, making customers wait too long, or other consequences. This simulation included coaching guidance and feedback via text—a coaching component helped learners who struggled with what to do next and provided feedback on mistakes.

It also included a game-like element of challenge: meters on the screen displayed the learner's speed and accuracy at all times, so the experience felt like a game—but in a realistic way, since the "game" measurements were the actual criteria that make for a good cashier—to be good at ringing up orders, you have to be fast and accurate.

Branching Simulations

The simulation model is in regular use today, though primarily in a limited form, once again because the authoring tools on the market currently facilitate the creation only of simple simulations. These authoring tool limitations can have quite a widespread effect: they cause many people in L&D departments to assume that simple simulations are all that can exist, period. There remains an opportunity for forward-thinking organizations to invest in more substantial learning experiences and expect a long-term payoff. Simulations in common use are generally in what's called the "branching" format, sometimes referred to as "choose your own adventure": learners watch a scene in video or animation, or read text describing the situation, and then are given a set of choices. For example, consider a situation in a retail store in which a customer approaches a salesperson on the retail floor and asks a question. The learner would then be asked to choose, from a set of choices, how the salesperson should respond. The storyline progresses—another video plays, for example—depending on the learner's decision. In other words, each decision leads to a different "branch," or path, of the potential storyline. Learners might receive feedback from the program if they make a mistake, or simply see an undesirable scene play out based on their choice, such as an angry customer.

Branching simulations can be realistic and effective; this method involves learners making realistic decisions that mirror those that they may need to make when performing their job. As with the design of any learning experience or any other type of design, the method alone doesn't guarantee effectiveness—the scenarios need to be meaningful and feel real to the learner, the decisions a learner is asked to make need to be nonobvious and require thought and understanding, and the feedback a learner receives should be detailed and help them understand, in a generalizable way, what they could have done better. Simple feedback saying "correct" or "incorrect" is not particularly helpful. But overall, this is a solid method to use, and one that can be created with a moderate amount of time and effort. More sophisticated simulations such as the Boston Chicken Cashier Trainer are more effective, and the approach is highly recommended, but these systems also require more time, budget, and skill to create and would require technical resources in today's world; current off-the-shelf authoring tools cannot create experiences of this complexity.

The "Watch, Rate, and Compare" Model

Another learning experience model that is often effective is the "Watch, Rate, and Compare" model, created by Kaleidoscope Learning back in 2002 (and described in Guralnick and Larson 2008). In this model, learners watch a video, rate the performance of the key person in the video, and compare their answers to those of experts and, in some cases, those of peers. For example, consider a professional development course for attorneys focused on helping the attorneys conduct interviews with new pro bono clients. There's an art to conducting these interviews in such a way that the attorneys gather all necessary information while—and due to—establishing a strong working relationship with their client. As part of this professional development course, attorneys are asked to watch a scenario in which an attorney conducts an interview, then rate the attorney's performance on key criteria. Finally, learners can compare their own ratings to those of experts, hear an expert explain why she rated the video attorney the way she did, and see the same situation again, handled well by the attorney. Figures 2.1–2.5 show screens from this sequence of events in one scenario, in which the attorney's client brings a third party, in this case the mother of her deceased fiancé, to the meeting, and the attorney must handle the situation appropriately while not allowing the mother, a third party whose presence could cause issues with confidentiality, among other things, to fully participate.

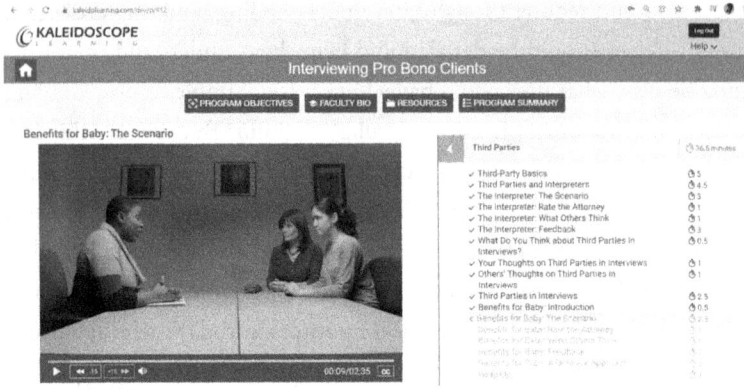

Figure 2.1 An Activity: Watching an initial scenario—An attorney, her client, and a third party

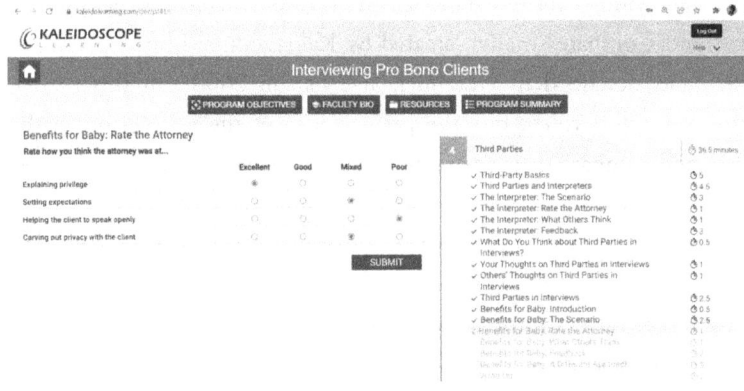

Figure 2.2 An Activity: Rating the attorney's performance

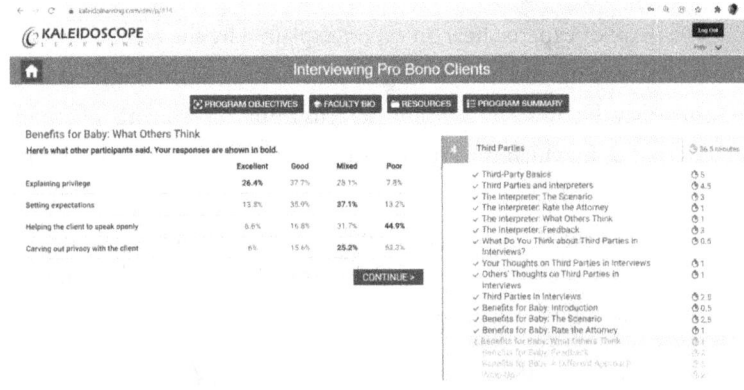

Figure 2.3 An Activity: Comparing your ratings to what others thought

Figure 2.4 An Activity: Getting feedback from the expert, in video

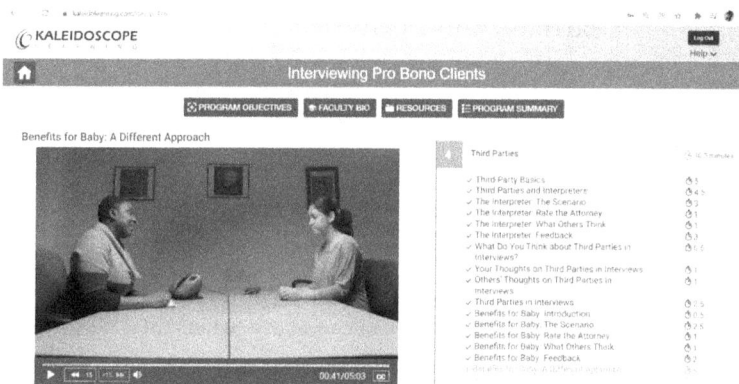

Figure 2.5 An Activity: Watching the scenario again, this time done well by the attorney

This method is an effective one and is particularly suited for skills in which a full-fledged simulation would be complex, at best, to create, such as one involving situations in which body language is critical (having a computer system read and evaluate a learner's body language is difficult at best using today's technology; asking the learner to evaluate an actor's body language in a video is useful and practical to produce).

Additional Activity Examples

The set of potential self-paced activities that a learning experience designer can create is limited, in theory, only by their imagination, though in practice is also limited by the capabilities of the software authoring tools on the market and by the level of skill and experience that a person has with a specific authoring tool. This is far from an ideal situation; my perspective is that learning designers should not be required to also have technical skills in order to be able to create online learning activities, the authoring tools should be designed in such a way that they support the creation of complex activities without requiring learning designers to think like programmers. But the current norm is that instructional designers within organizations are able to use off-the-shelf authoring tools to create some reasonably complex activities that are customized to the content and goals.

Microlearning, Workflow and "Just-In-Time" Learning, and Performance Support

While online courses still make up the majority of online learning in organizations, the industry is currently undergoing a substantial shift away from larger, "monolithic" courses and toward more flexible models that allow greater learner control. A currently trendy term for smaller learning experiences, much smaller than courses, is *microlearning* (Association for Talent Development 2021); while it's often a good idea to replace courses with smaller experiences that learners can access when they need them, based on their goals and needs, smaller experiences aren't always better—some skills or content areas, for particular audiences, need more direction and more of an in-depth experience. Microlearning as a term can refer to experiences that are valuable and effective and also to those that are not.

A related concept is that of *workflow learning* (Cross 2004), the idea that employees can be provided with ways to access information and training that they need in a "just-in-time" way, within their natural workflow. This model differs substantially from the traditional model of "upfront" training, in which people are expected to complete all training before beginning a role, and allows employees much more control of their learning and development. A good workflow learning process makes substantial use of smaller components—reference information, how-to videos, brief training pieces, and more—that can help employees accomplish a task when they are ready to do so, or "just in time," and without removing them from their natural workflow.

One final relevant concept is a term that never has quite caught on as much as it should, that of *performance support* (Gery 2001; Rossett and Schafer 2007). This term refers to products that help employees perform their jobs better—more efficiently, accurately, and easily—and are used just-in-time, when the employee needs them. Performance support doesn't necessarily need to be high-tech; for example, a cashier in a small store might tape an index card to the cash register with key things to know about how to ring up a transaction. The cashier could then refer to the card in the process of ringing up a customer, so this would be in the context of their workflow and also very much "just-in-time." Now, such a card wouldn't necessarily be a "learning" experience—it would help the cashier perform better rather than directly helping them learn (though over a period of time, the cashier would likely learn many of the things on the card). Performance support can be much more complex, taking various forms—anything from an easily searchable information reference (e.g., Target's *Eureka*! information reference, described in Guralnick and Larson 2008) to a system that helps people better use a complex piece of software (e.g., Christensen 2009) to a sophisticated system that helps the user make decisions; this concept has been explored for years in the form of artificial intelligence-based *expert systems* (see, for example, Feigenbaum and Buchanan 1993) that were first used in the medical field.

Collaborative Learning

To this point, we've focused on virtual classes, which are *synchronous*—everyone takes the class at the same time—and self-paced learning and performance support, which are *asynchronous*—each employee does the work on their own schedule, often driven by their personal goals and needs. There's also a significant role for collaborative learning outside of a class or virtual class setting. Collaborative learning can take place in a number of ways and is typically informal.

Social Networks

Many organizations use Microsoft's Office suite, which now has incorporated Yammer, which is essentially a corporate version of Facebook. Microsoft Teams includes collaborative features as well, and Microsoft may phase out Yammer over time and integrate it into Teams, though there are currently uses for both: Yammer for open, organization wide discussions, and Teams for specific work teams to work together in closed groups (Branscombe 2020). Open, company wide collaborative software, from any vendor, provides employees with a way to reach others in the organization to ask questions, share information, form relationships, and have informal conversations. Such collaboration across geographic and time boundaries can be immensely helpful and has been of particular use during the pandemic as all employees worked remotely. Another popular collaboration method is via Slack, an application that allows teams to work together easily via a running conversation. We'll cover specific collaboration software options in more detail in Chapter 3.

One challenge an organization faces regarding the use of social media is that of structure. Conversations that are open to all employees are great, but especially in a large organization, can become unwieldy or simply can be drowned out by the massive amount of information on a social network, and there may not be an incentive or reason for employees to participate. Organizations may want to create topic-based groups to help employees better find relevant conversations, as one approach.

Communities of Practice

An ideal way to use social networks within an organization is to support employees in working with others to form a *community of practice* (CoP) (see Lave and Wenger 1991; a detailed example of a community of practice in use in an advertising agency can be found in Christina Merl's 2009 publication), defined by Lave and Wenger as a group of people who "share a concern or a passion for something they do and learn how to do it better as they interact regularly." CoPs within a work environment certainly have the capability to improve individual and team performance and to continue to build a learning culture within an organization.

Blended Approaches to Learning

One key characteristic of nearly any large-scale learning initiative is that as critical as technology is in today's learning experiences, technology must serve the needs and goals of the audience, rather than making demands of them. Along these lines, *blended* approaches to learning are becoming more and more commonly used, in which a learning experience makes use of different technologies or, frequently, a mix of technology-based and non-technology-based learning. Blended approaches can come in nearly any format and can also mix formal and informal learning.

Common E-Learning Experience Types: A Summary

Table 2.1 summarizes the common types of learning experiences and their key advantages, disadvantages, and best uses.

Table 2.1 Common e-learning experience types and their best uses

Type	Pros	Cons	Best for...
Virtual classes	• Easy and fast to set up technically; • Direct, personal interaction and discussions are possible	• Passive learning experience if the group is large	• Small groups with an experienced instructor/leader; • Content that can be best learned via discussion more than doing (though virtual classes can be combined with other activities)
Massive Open Online Courses (MOOCs)	• Platforms exist for fairly easy technical setup and many existing MOOCs are available at little or no cost; • Much of the content is pre-planned and pre-recorded, so MOOCs can provide some interaction at a minimal cost	• Can be fairly passive learning experiences overall; • Easy for learners to participate only minimally	• Large audiences; • Cases in which a useful MOOC already exists, so an organization doesn't need to create anything new

(Continued)

Table 2.1 (Continued)

Read/Watch/Test	• Simple and inexpensive to create and to produce technically; • Provide a clear evaluation score (though not always a score that is useful)	• Passive experiences; • Learning is too easily minimal and covers facts more than thinking and analysis skills	• Situations in which you need to create something quickly and inexpensively; • Areas in which you have, or can easily produce, compelling videos, often from experts
Traditional e-learning activities and assessments (such as matching, multiple choices, and drag-and-drop)	• Simple and inexpensive to create and to produce technically; • Familiar format to most learners based on their experiences in school	• Less-than-ideal learning and assessment experiences; • Focus on facts and recognition rather than skills and reasoning	• Situations in which you need to create something fairly quickly and inexpensively; • Content that is unavoidably more fact-based, such as content for compliance purposes
Learn-by-doing simulations	• Can be powerful, engaging, and realistic; • Facilitate the transfer of skills to the job by providing experience in a safe environment	• Relatively expensive to produce; • Require a relatively high level of skill to create and script	• Particularly well-suited for tasks in which there's a defined procedure, and for simpler social skills; • Usually an excellent method when there's a need for training and sufficient budget or an ROI argument to be made
"Watch, Rate, and Compare" activities	• Engaging and realistic; • Reinforce key performance criteria of a job role	• Less immersive than simulations; • A bit more difficult to produce than simple watch/read learning	• Excellent for social situations where the learner can benefit from watching and modeling their behavior

Microlearning, workflow and "just-in-time" learning, and performance support	• Fit within an employee's workflow rather than removing them from the job for learning; • Increase efficiency and performance	• Some job roles or content areas need more depth than these models provide; • Designing these experiences can be a new experience for some people; • It can be a challenge to make sure that target audience members remember that they have these products available	• Specifics depend on the situation, but this is a category that is worth considering in almost all situations
Social networks	• Can be used whenever employees need them, within their workflow; • Can facilitate collaboration among employees at different levels and in different locations	• Discussions can be unfocused; • Particular content or answers can be difficult to find easily; • The accuracy and perspective of posts are not vetted	• Often a great augmentation to other methods of learning
Communities of practice	• Facilitate collaboration, typically long-term as well as short-term; • Fosters the generation of new and creative ideas	• Can be labor-intensive in terms of both time and thought; • Not always easy to make these happen	• An excellent addition when you have the right team

Underlying Themes of Good Online Learning Design

Whichever technologies a learning experience uses, the key to a good learning experience lies in its *design*. Design in this context refers not only to the look and graphic design but to the overall experience, at all levels. The concept of *user-centered design*, often credited to design and user experience expert Don Norman (Norman 2002), is critical in the design of learning experiences. This concept is defined as "an iterative design process in which designers focus on the users and their needs in each phase of the design process" (Interaction Design Foundation 2021). In the world of online learning, this means starting the process of designing a learning experience around the audience and goals (Guralnick 2019), and creating an experience, and specific content, to help learners achieve their goals. This approach differs substantially from the common approach of identifying content topics and details and explaining them to learners; instead, a good design process focuses on the learners' needs and goals: what do they need to learn to do? What types of experiences will they appreciate and connect with emotionally? What's their workflow like and how can an experience fit into it? The answers to these questions, among others, can inform the design of a great learning experience.

There are a number of themes that are found in most successful learning experiences and can serve as high-level design guidelines. Those are learner control, coaching guidance and feedback, the use of stories and scenarios, the right types of interactivity, and the use of a respectful style, tone, and language. We cover those in more detail in the following sections.

Learner Control

Traditional e-learning, like much of traditional classroom education and training, tends to put the course or instructor in control—the learner's role is to do what is asked of them. In many online learning courses today, learners are given something to read or watch on-screen and then asked to take quizzes, typically called "knowledge checks" in organizational learning settings. This model leaves the learner in the position of simply following, or "navigating through" the course in a very minimal sense (often just clicking a button labeled NEXT or CONTINUE in order to progress through the course's educational content). Learners often don't find this type of experience to be engaging and tend to do them grudgingly because the experience is not enjoyable and doesn't seem relevant—never in their job will most employees need to recite information, they'll need to perform skills. Finally, and perhaps most critically, traditional e-learning puts the learner in the position of not feeling valued or respected, just by the nature of the experience.

Better-designed online learning experiences, and learning experiences in general, allow the learner to be *in control*. This can take the form of putting a learner in a realistic simulation and letting them decide how to solve a complex problem, by giving them a decision aid to help them when they need it on the job (and when they choose to use it), by providing connections with other employees whose experience can be helpful, or in many other ways, some of which we have explored earlier. Learner control is a key underlying theme to keep in mind when it comes to designing a learning experience.

Coaching Guidance and Feedback

Another key theme is that of *coaching*. Coaching is widely accepted as an ideal part of in-person experiences; sports teams have coaches, and teachers or experienced coworkers often are asked to play the role of a coach in some form. Coaching is equally critical in an online experience. Online coaching can sometimes take the form of an actual person, via either synchronous (e.g., a Zoom call) or asynchronous (e.g., e-mail, Slack interactions, text messages, etc.) interactions. But coaching can also be built into online experiences in more automated, but nonetheless helpful, ways. A high-end example of this would be using artificial intelligence techniques to create a coaching component that has a realistic "chat" in text with a learner; a simpler example might be building in a coaching character who the learner can ask a set of in-context questions of, and who can provide feedback on the learner's decisions and performance in a course. Coaching in the form of both *guidance* (helping a learner decide what to do next) and *feedback* (providing thoughts on a learner's work, either on a specific decision or response or on a pattern of responses, often including whether their decisions were good or bad, but definitely not limited to that) is critical to a good learning experience.

The Use of Stories and Scenarios

Traditional instructional models often focus on information, with the goal of getting people to memorize information—for example, a U.S. history course might have a section on, say, the War of 1812, and ask students to learn the dates and locations of key battles. That's certainly relevant information, but what's really critical to learn is the stories—everything from what caused the conflict to dramatic personal stories of key figures. Stories provide detail and realism, and also tend to be compelling and memorable (Boris 2017). Even the best-intentioned students or employees tend to tune out volumes of factual information, or can't process it all, while stories are easier to follow and to relate to other experiences.

In an organizational learning setting, stories can play a critical role in a learning experience. For example, an online retail training program that my company, Kaleidoscope Learning, created for use by people who were interested in preparing themselves for a sales role in a retail store, included a section that was built around realistic sales situations and objections that a salesperson in a retail store may encounter. People taking the course were shown realistic situations in which customers approached a salesperson in video. These *scenarios* were based on real-life experiences and stories from actual retail salespeople who were candid about what challenges they faced, and what worked and what didn't.

Actual stories can work well directly, too. For example: in a scenario-based sales program, learners might also be able to see stories in text or video in which salespeople directly tell their success and failure stories and explain what worked well or poorly and why. A particularly effective use of stories is to work them into a scenario-based experience—for example, a salesperson in the retail course I described earlier might make a poor decision in their interaction with the online customer, which is then an ideal time for them to see a story about a similar situation that someone faced in real life.

Even in a simple lecture format, stories can work fantastically well; an expert sharing stories about their experiences is often compelling. For example, parts of a professional development course we created at Kaleidoscope Learning for an audience of attorneys on working with pro bono clients (Guralnick and Kinnamon 2018) include an experienced pro bono attorney discussing her experiences. A traditional lecture might have the expert listing things to do—for example, "make sure your clients schedule a follow-up meeting"; this course included a story from the expert about how she once inadvertently caused a client to schedule a follow-up meeting at a time that they could not comfortably make, by phrasing things in a way that made the meeting time sound like more of a demand than intended. This story was interesting, compelling, and memorable—and was realistic, a true example of the kind of thing that someone taking the course might experience on the job. In all ways, such an example is much more valuable than simply telling people information.

The Right Types of Interactivity

The concept of *interactivity* in online learning—providing experiences in which learners do something rather than solely sitting and watching or reading—is another key underlying theme. The key to successful interactive learning experiences is to build activities and interactions around meaningful decisions that the learner is asked to make. The idea is to embed interactivity into the design approach. Some common forms of interactivity, such as dragging and dropping answers to questions, are not particularly effective or meaningful. In contrast, an activity for an audience of warehouse workers (this example is from a course that Kaleidoscope Learning created for a nonprofit foundation that delivers courses for the retail industry) in which the employee needs to arrange a trailer optimally by dragging different-sized boxes to their ideal spots in an on-screen trailer is a realistic task—they have to load trailers optimally on the job—works well since the interactivity is meaningful and relevant.

Game-based learning approaches also are most effective when they are meaningful. The Boston Chicken Cashier Trainer that we explored earlier includes key game-like elements, most notably scores and the element of challenge, as part of a realistic task, ringing up customer orders. In contrast, a *Jeopardy!*-style game in which a learner needs to recall information might be fun but is unlikely to provide realistic learning that transfers to skill performance.

Respectful Tone, Style, and Language

There's a tendency for online learning experiences to follow the tone of traditional childhood education, in which the course, in the form of text or a narrator, essentially treats the learner as if the course is the expert, the learner is a novice, and the learner must follow instructions. Progressive educational theories dating back to John Dewey (Dewey 1938) argue, quite convincingly, that this is not an ideal approach to follow in children's education, and if anything, it's less successful and less appropriate in the context of adult learning.

Further, forward-thinking organizations look for ways to make their employees feel valued and appreciated; providing learning and performance support experiences that treat employees respectfully, by providing applicable, useful content and activities, and using collegial language that doesn't talk down to the employees, can separate themselves and improve their cultures.

Summary

Online learning can take various forms, from live, instructor-led formats to a variety of self-paced learning and performance experiences, and everything in between. In this chapter, we have covered a variety of approaches and discussed some of the advantages and uses of each. One of the critical challenges to address as an organization is to focus on learning experiences that follow the themes in the previous section as much as possible, toward the goal of creating a culture that's designed to help employees perform well and feel valued. In the following chapter, we'll take a look at different ways to create or purchase online learning experiences.

CHAPTER 3

Learning Technology

Courses, Content, and Experiences

Introduction

The world of learning technologies is tremendously varied, consisting of off-the-shelf courses; tools to create custom courses and experiences; outside vendors and subcontractors; software to create components of courses, such as images and interactive videos; systems to manage and track content and learner performance; and a variety of other technologies. In this chapter, we'll examine the various options and discuss reasons an organization might want to employ each option, and the contexts in which each is likely to be a good fit.

Course/Experience Creation and Acquisition

In the last chapter, we took a look at the various types of online learning experiences and how to best employ them. Another key decision is how these experiences are designed and developed—who creates them? Organizations typically include a mix of the following creation methods:

- An *in-house Learning & Development team*, often using an off-the-shelf authoring tool (software that allows people to build online learning experiences, generally self-paced experiences, without being a computer programmer) along with other software to create images, animations, and videos. This method has the advantage of typically being relatively inexpensive, since the work is done by in-house resources, and also can leverage an in-house team's understanding of the audience, goals, and content.

- *User-generated content* from employees. This approach uses social tools to allow, and encourage, employees to post their own advice, examples, and more. Most organizations use systems that allow internal L&D managers to vet user-generated content, and/or provide different levels of posting permissions for different users (Baron 2019). Supporting user-generated content leverages the expertise of employees and can help encourage a learning culture.

- *An outside company or subcontractor.* There's an entire industry of online learning companies that have the resources to create online learning experiences. The level of quality varies; most of the companies in this space that have been around for a while can produce courses that look great and professional, though it's much more difficult to find companies (as it is with subcontractors or employees) who understand how to create truly effective learning experiences. We'll cover how to select and work with an outside "vendor" company in detail in Chapter 5. Hiring an outside company or subcontractor comes with a cost but can allow an organization not only to expand its resource set but also to create learning experiences that it may not be able to produce, at least not at the same level of quality, in-house.

- *Off-the-shelf courses or course libraries.* There are a variety of existing courses and learning experiences available, typically for purchase though occasionally for free. One of the major trade-offs in deciding whether and where to consider using existing outside courses and experiences is that of cost versus applicability; acquiring an outside course will nearly invariably be less expensive than creating one, but in many situations, outside courses are too generic, don't feel relevant to an organization's target audience, or don't fit the style and culture that an organization is looking for.

Technologies for Live Presentations and Class Sessions

More than ever since the beginning of the COVID-19 pandemic, instructor-led classes have moved online, using technologies such as Zoom.

There are a number of popular software-as-a-service (SaaS) platforms that can be used for smaller online classes, meetings, and discussions, all of which offer live video meeting capabilities and other features. There are also similar software platforms that are better suited for larger audiences, such as those in a large class, a webinar, or a conference. Below, we take a look at some of the major options, though this market and the specific features of the products, do change frequently.

Zoom: This rapidly became the best-known online meeting platform as the pandemic began and it became the de facto standard for schools to use. Zoom allows video meetings and works well for small online classes. Zoom has a "breakout rooms" feature that allows classes to break up into even smaller groups, typically for the purposes of separate discussions, which many instructors like to use. Zoom's standard meeting features such as screen sharing are easy to use, and Zoom makes it easy to record meetings (either locally or in the cloud) for later posting and viewing. As of this writing, Zoom has a shareable whiteboard feature as well, though it's somewhat limited. New versions and upgrades to Zoom roll out frequently.

Adobe Connect: This is another platform in common use today, particularly because it's from Adobe, the well-known provider of Acrobat, Photoshop, Premiere, and other programs that are in wide use. Adobe Connect's features are, for the most part, similar to Zoom's, though as with Zoom, new and improved features are released frequently in today's competitive market.

WebEx: Perhaps the first well-known virtual meeting platform, Webex is still in wide use today. It is similar to Zoom and Adobe Connect in terms of features, though as of this writing, feels a bit less modern to use.

Microsoft Teams: Microsoft has continued to expand its Teams software, which is frequently used for video meetings and also includes document collaboration features (similar to those of Google Docs) and messaging channels (similar to those of Slack); we will cover Google Docs and Slack later in this chapter.

There are a variety of other products in this space; GoToMeeting is another longtime platform, and BlueJeans is a platform that has been growing in popularity and was recently, as of this writing, acquired by Verizon.

Most virtual training platforms offer a "webinar" version as well as a standard version. The primary difference between these two versions is typically that the webinar versions are intended to focus more on the presenter than on discussion, with the idea that these are best suited for large classes and for large conference sessions.

Technologies for Collaboration and Communication

Technologies for collaboration and communication are not specifically for learning but are key elements of informal learning and performance and therefore merit discussion here. Three key types of relevant technologies are:

- *Document collaboration*: These systems allow people to work on documents together, including communicating about the documents via comments. The standard version of document collaboration resembles Microsoft Word's comments and change tracking features, but on the Web so people can work on a document simultaneously and without sending the document around and keeping track of versions. Google Docs is a common documentation collaboration platform, and Microsoft Teams' similar features are taking over within many organizations.
- *Messaging channels*: Slack emerged as the popular messaging system; teams of people can use Slack to message others in the group via a "channel"—for example, you might create a Slack channel for a particular project. Particularly now that people often work remotely, messaging channels are a nice way to communicate and also learn informally. Microsoft Teams includes channel features that are similar to those of Slack.
- *Social networking platforms*: Yammer, now owned by Microsoft, emerged as the social network standard within most organizations, essentially serving as a "Facebook for organizations." For learning purposes, this is a useful way to reach out to large groups to find information or advice.

Creating Courses and Content In-House

Earlier, we discussed a variety of approaches to online learning, and the idea that creating self-paced online experiences are often created by in-house learning and development personnel. But what type of team structures can work best within an organization? And what software tools should they use?

Design and Development Team

The definition of an "instructional designer," particularly one who produces online learning, has evolved significantly in recent years. This role was formerly viewed as someone who would gather content from a subject matter expert and, more than anything, organize and format the content into a traditional instructional experience. Organizations have moved in recent years to a much more performance-oriented approach to learning, and the role of an instructional designer is evolving into that of a "learning experience designer," a much broader and more varied role than in the past.

While my own view is that the e-learning industry is in need of better software tools that allow learning experience designers to focus more on design and content and less on technical implementation than they do today, current instructional designers are typically asked to be jacks of many trades and to possess not only expertise in educational design, but in creating graphics, animations, and videos, and using off-the-shelf authoring tools, software that allows people to create online learning without being a computer programmer (though most current tools do require a fair amount of technical skill, particularly if the goal is to create something more than a minimal learner experience).

It is certainly possible, and can be advisable, to create a team of people who are a bit more specialized. A small such team might include the following roles:

- A learning experience designer who does not do the implementation but designs the experiences serves as the lead connection to the subject matter experts (in whatever form that may take—often people to speak with but sometimes things to read or watch), creates specifications, and reviews and supervises the work.

- A graphic designer who creates screen mockups and images under the guidance of the learning experience designer.
- Other specialists as needed, such as people who can create illustrations, animations, and videos, again under the guidance of the learning experience designer.
- An authoring tool expert who plays an implementation role, building the course or content in the tool by following the design specifications and incorporating the images, videos, and other assets created by others on the team.

Even under a specialization model, ideally all team members can contribute to the overall quality of the experience, and some of the work will certainly involve people working together in groups or teams. In practice, it's fairly common for individual learning experience designers to take on all of the above roles and create a product on their own. This approach is usually best suited for smaller projects.

Whatever the team size, it's ideal to have people review and test a course who are not part of the design and development team, and to include members of the target audience in the review, as well as others who are experienced in quality assurance (QA) and can catch typos and clearly report any technical bugs.

Process

There are a handful of common learning design and development models, though in online learning, there are often advantages to prototyping a portion of a learning experience in order to get feedback fairly early on. A few things to generally keep in mind regarding virtually any e-learning design and development process are:

- Take the time to clearly understand the content, goals, and target audience upfront, including understanding how the target audience might use a learning product within their workflow. (Sometimes, the in-house instructional team doubles as subject matter experts and has a leg up on this process.)

- Involve members of the target audience at various stages of the project for review and feedback, as much as is possible and practical.
- Ideal learning experiences are typically created by experts in learning design but with input feedback from subject matter experts (SMEs) and members of the target audience.

E-Learning Authoring Tools

E-learning courses, and sometimes other digital content, is typically created using off-the-shelf authoring tools, which allow instructional designers and subject matter experts to create courses without needing to learn computer programming. Now, these tools are far from a magic bullet, in several ways: first, there's an art to creating a great learning experience, and that falls on the design and development team; second, the more powerful authoring tools do ask users to at least think technically, so implementing a course in most authoring tools is a semitechnical job today; and third, today's authoring tools are fairly limited in what they can produce—they were designed with a more traditional learning methodology in mind. My view is that in order for online learning to reach its potential on a large scale, one thing that needs to happen is for the authoring tools to be radically improved, both in terms of their ease of use and in terms of the experiences they can support. In today's world, common authoring tools to know include the following:

- *Articulate Storyline*: This is currently considered the most widely used e-learning authoring tool. It's based on a "slide" model, using a concept that instructional designers are certainly familiar with, as in PowerPoint, but this structure also implicitly encourages the design of training that follows a traditional page-turning/quiz model. Storyline allows people with a bit of technical skill to create some reasonably sophisticated activities and includes features that support the development process, such as a tool to accept and track feedback from people reviewing the course as it's being developed. Most instructional designers today are experienced in Storyline, though as the authoring tool market improves, instructional designers should no longer need to be so familiar with any particular software product. Storyline produces output in SCORM format—this is the common standard format used by learning management systems (LMSs), which we'll discuss in the next chapter—so Storyline courses can be housed in any standard LMS.

- *Adobe Captivate*: This is another popular authoring tool, originally focusing on capturing screens from software programs to help people learn how to use them. It also allows the creation of simple branching scenarios along with quizzes and produces LMS-compatible SCORM output.
- *Lectora*: Another SCORM-course creation tool that has been around for a long time, this tool is simpler for beginners to use than Storyline and Captivate but also more limited in the experiences that it can produce.

There are a number of other authoring tools that create SCORM courses, and a growing number of alternative approaches to course creation that cannot necessarily be hosted in an LMS. This area is evolving and forward-thinking organizations would do well to move beyond simpler learning experiences to consider a variety of advanced approaches. The authoring tool market will likely continue to evolve significantly over time.

Additional Software Tools

Online learning designers in today's world often are asked to create media and images on their own. Some teams have graphics, animation, and video specialists, which is very helpful, and teams will occasionally outsource media work to subcontractors or vendor companies, depending on the timing needs and available budget. Commonly used tools by instructional designers for media creation include the following:

- *Graphic design tools*: Adobe Photoshop is considered the standard for graphics and photo editing work. Adobe Illustrator is a bit more complex and, as the name suggests, generally better when graphics work involves drawing. There are numerous other graphics packages, including some good products that are available at no charge, including Paint.net (a graphics design tool) and Canva (a graphics site for nongraphic artists that's based on templates) as well.

- *Video editing tools*: TechSmith's Camtasia is a very popular software application in the e-learning world. It allows video recording, simple video editing, and the creation of videos from images and audio files. Camtasia also includes some transition effects and the ability to include simple questions along with a SCORM export option. Adobe Premiere and other video editing programs are a bit more sophisticated and may be more difficult to learn.
- *Animation tools*: Vyond, formerly GoAnimate, has emerged as the leader in e-learning animation software, since it comes with built-in templates and characters that make it relatively fast and easy to create nice-looking animations, while still providing a fair amount of creative control to the user. There are also a number of programs that are more labor-intensive and require more artistic skill and time to produce animations; those are more commonly used by animation specialists rather than by e-learning designers.

Online Learning on Different Devices

More than ever, organizational learning takes place anytime, anywhere; just-in-time learning and performance support products—products that help employees *perform* a task rather than necessarily helping them learn a skill—are designed to be used by employees wherever they are, and whenever they need them. Allowing employees to use learning and performance products on mobile phones and tablets, as well as on laptops and desktops, is often critical.

Most authoring tools create courses and content that follow responsive design, meaning that they will look reasonable on larger and smaller devices. Ideally, however, experiences can be designed to make appropriate use of a particular device type and the context in which they will be used. For example, salespeople working on their laptops might enjoy, and learn from, a realistic, immersive, game-like sales training simulation in which they practice selling to realistic customers, who appear in video. But such a game may not translate well to a smaller screen. On the other hand, a salesperson who's on their way to a meeting with a potential customer might benefit from a mobile phone app that lists key objections that other salespeople in the same division have encountered, and how they overcame them. The key is to consider the entire use context when designing an experience.

The widespread adoption of mobile devices has caused a significant practical change within most organizations' IT practices; it was once common for organizations to restrict access to their intranet and other internal applications to people who were working on computers that were on the company network and usually that were owned by the organization and set up by the organization's IT department. It has become much more common now to allow employees to work from their own devices; this is often referred to as a BYOD—Bring Your Own Device—model.

New Technologies and Approaches to Online Learning and Performance

New technologies are rapidly emerging, and many new technologies have the potential to have a great impact on learning and performance, if employed wisely. The key, once again, is to design experiences that make use of the context in which a technology will be used and also take advantage of the capabilities of the technology. A mobile app might make use of its awareness of a user's location by showing relevant, location-specific information—for example, an app for maintenance technicians might tell them the location of the nearest store that has a particular part in stock.

Technologies such as virtual reality (VR), augmented reality (AR), artificial intelligence (AI), wearable technologies, and others are becoming more affordable and more mainstream. Each of these technologies offers the potential to improve learning and performance. We'll cover these technologies and others in more detail in Chapter 9.

Summary

In this chapter, we have explored some of the common tools and technologies often used by instructional designers and discussed the various ways that organizations can create learning experiences. The options are varied and often change, and there's an opportunity for forward-thinking organizations to move away from some of the traditional approaches to online learning to create a new culture around learning and performance, and to use technology in ways that employees find to be truly helpful and relevant. This chapter provided an overview of the current state of the world, along with some thoughts on how it can be improved.

CHAPTER 4

Learning Technology

Learning Management and Administration

For quite a number of years, learning management systems (LMSs) have been the standard way for organizations to host, deliver, and track, and report on employee learning. An LMS typically serves as the "front end" website by which employees access their learning experiences, often providing a curriculum of recommended courses as well as tracking learner completion and scores. From the organizational side, an LMS provides an organization with a way to deliver online learning to their employees, providing not only a place for the learning experience to "live" but also tracking which employees have accessed various learning options and how they have performed. There are pros and cons to the standard LMS approach, and the world of possibilities and related software is evolving. First, it's worth a moment to go over the concepts that underlie the ability of employees to access online learning and of organizations to monitor it. The key concepts to be familiar with are the following:

- *Hosting*: Online learning experiences and courses are, at their technical core, computer programs (or, more specifically, "web applications") that run on a website. These typically take one of several forms: custom-coded programs that reside on, or are "hosted" by, an organization's own servers or the servers at an outside vendor (such as Amazon Web Services (AWS), Google Cloud, or Microsoft Azure, as examples); courses created in an online platform, such as Coursera or edX; or, most commonly, as courses that are created using specific "authoring tool" software and then run in a learning management system (LMS), which itself is a web application that an organization has installed either on its own servers or on outside servers such as Amazon Web Services and others.

- *Delivery*: This term refers to how employees, the end-users, access a course or product. This can be done directly on an outside vendor's website but is commonly done using an organization's intranet or, particularly, the LMS—employees often log in to the LMS and access courses from there. Employees may be asked to follow a specific curriculum, as set by a manager or administrator, or to take certain courses based on their experience level or past performance. Or employees can search for courses to take. The specifics, and the employees' experiences and levels of satisfaction, depend on the particular design and features of the LMS and the way the courses have been organized by the managers and administrators.

- *User Data Tracking*: Most courses provide a way for an organization to track each user's performance, at least to the level of whether they have completed a course and their performance on any assessments, such as quizzes or exams. This data needs to be tracked in a database in some form, which can be custom-coded or part of a system. One of the key capabilities of LMSs is that they provide the ability to track user data for courses that they host; LMSs only can host courses created in certain technical formats—SCORM (which stands for Sharable Content Object Reference Model) is an old standard but still the most commonly used, and xAPI (also sometimes known as the Experience API or the Tin Can API) is a newer, more flexible standard—but can track certain user data for courses in those formats. For non-LMS courses, data tracking (which data is tracked) depends entirely on the code or the system used and can be anywhere from minimal to substantial.

- *Reporting*: Related to data tracking is the notion of reporting; LMSs provide a variety of ways for training administrators to view employees' progress and completion status on each course, any assessment scores, and sometimes other information. As with data tracking, reporting for non-LMS courses depends on the code or system used.

- *Administration*: Training administrators have the ability to add, remove, and update courses, to assign access to courses to specific employees or groups of employees, and perform other administrative functions.

The idea behind LMSs is to provide a central place for all online courses, and for user data tracking, reporting, and course delivery. In order to make that manageable, LMSs require courses to be built to either the older SCORM standard or the newer xAPI standard (or occasionally another older standard, AICC), so that the LMS program can communicate with the course code to launch the course, track user progress, restore user progress when someone accesses a course (i.e., the program remembers where the user was in the course), and save data for reporting, all in the same format.

The SCORM and xAPI standards

The primary standard for e-learning courses has been, and currently still is, SCORM. SCORM was first developed by the U.S. government's Advanced Distributed Learning (ADL) initiative in 2000 (Rustici Software 2000) and was later revised, with the current, and presumably final, version being SCORM 2004, 4th edition. This version was released in 2004 yet is still in wide use today. A useful analogy from Rustici Software, a company that specializes in SCORM conformance and has its own LMS, is that SCORM for e-learning courses is analogous to DVD standards that allowed DVDs to play on any standard DVD player, regardless of the manufacturer (SCORM.com 2021). This analogy holds quite well, both in terms of the strengths—easy interoperability, SCORM files will generally play and support user data tracking on any SCORM-compliant LMS—and weaknesses, in that a wide variety of innovative learning experiences cannot be created in a SCORM compliant file, or not easily, in the way that DVDs only supported minimal, specific types of interactivity and nothing more. We'll discuss these limitations in more detail in the next section.

The experience API, or "xAPI," standard is, again using the Rustici Software explanation for reference, "a new specification for learning technology that makes it possible to collect data about the wide range of experiences a person has (online and offline)" (Rustici Software 2021). API stands for "application programming interface," the usual term used to describe how web applications share data with each other. xAPI records are produced in a much more general format than SCORM data and are intended to take a large step beyond SCORM to allow the tracking of experiences in the classroom, via online discussions, and more (Torrance 2021). As of this writing, uses of xAPI are growing and evolving, but SCORM is still the predominant standard.

Limitations of LMSs

A major trade-off when it comes to implementing a standard of almost any kind is that the standard necessarily brings with it limitations. LMSs handle only courses and products that were created in SCORM or xAPI format (or possibly in a very old standard called AICC), which significantly limits the types of learner experiences that can be created. SCORM courses also are created as a single, large .zip file and stored in the LMS, which works well for the purposes of having everything clearly in one location but is also limiting: sophisticated web applications often rely on database programs that are not supported via LMSs, plus by forcing an entire course to be in a single file, any updates or changes necessitate a potentially time-consuming change process. For example, suppose that a course hosted on a web platform that is not a traditional LMS, such as Coursera or others (including Kaleidoscope Learning's Encompass platform, which hosts several of the courses referenced in this book) needs one video to be updated—there's been a small content change, or fix, and the old video needs to be replaced. On such a web platform, this process generally requires simply replacing the video and publishing it so that it's available to all learners; the process is quick and nothing unnecessary is changed. In a SCORM course created by an off-the-shelf authoring tool, which covers nearly all SCORM courses, changing a video involves replacing the video in the authoring tool software and then re-exporting the entire course (which can be time-consuming as the major tools need time to re-compress all videos in the course) to produce a new, replacement SCORM .zip file. These files can be large and the entire process can be a bit cumbersome.

Overall, my view of LMSs and the SCORM standard is that they risk limiting people's views of what online learning experiences can be. The norm, for practical reasons, is to use an off-the-shelf tool to create a SCORM file, starting with the constraints rather than with the goals, which is not an ideal design process. Also, and critically, the set of learning experiences that can be created using today's off-the-shelf authoring tools is limited and not always ideal. Another limitation is that current LMS reporting tends to focus on tracking learner progress, which is helpful but misses other opportunities, such as tracking data that can lead to improvements in the products themselves or identify misconceptions that people may have about their roles. For example, Eureka!, a performance support product created for Target Stores by Kaleidoscope Learning on its Encompass platform (Guralnick and Larson 2008) included a search feature and tracked a variety of data including searches that were unsuccessful—meaning that the user did not choose any of the results (even if there were search results). This feature uncovered something interesting: one group at Target, those who worked on the sales floor, were searching for a term called "chargebacks" in their customized system; this term refers to items that have been returned to the store and then need to be sent back to the manufacturer or distributor. Sales floor team members' official job roles, according to headquarters, did not involve chargebacks, so there was nothing relevant in their system about the concept, just a few peripherally related pages of information. But as it turned out, people in the sales floor role believed that they did need to be involved in this process; this disconnect was surfaced only by the Encompass platform's reporting and tracking and resulted in additions to the Eureka! system and changes to the job description. This is an example of the types of small but significant data that a well-designed system can uncover, going far beyond simple user progress or tracking, and represents a forward-thinking, holistic approach to learning and performance.

Learning Experience Platforms

Learning experience platforms (LXPs) are considered logical successors to LMSs. While LMSs tend to be focused on courses and sometimes on curricula, LXPs look to broaden a learner's range of experiences to include *user-generated content*—typically information created by the target audience members themselves, such as social media comments and user-created blog posts—and external content from the Web, outside the organization, along with internal courses, with the goal of adding informal learning to formal course learning. Degreed was perhaps the earliest LXP pioneer, and major LMS providers such as Cornerstone have augmented their offerings and marketed them as LXPs as well. Some systems, such as EdCast, view their products as supporting people in their careers as a whole. Overall, the positioning of LXPs, which vary in nature, is to move the focus from the employer-centric administration focus of an LMS to a more employee-centric model (Bersin 2019).

Learning Analytics

The term *learning analytics*, according to the Society for Learning Analytics Research (SOLAR), refers to "the measurement, collection, analysis and reporting of data about learners and their contexts" (SOLAR 2021), with the data being used for the purposes of improving learning, both for specific learners and in the aggregate, by using data to improve the design of future learning experiences. Learning experience platforms are beginning to take advantage of learning analytics, but there is much more that can be done in the future. There's currently a large amount of research being conducted involving learning analytics; as one significant example, Dr. Ryan Baker's Penn Center for Learning Analytics (www.upenn.edu/learninganalytics), at the University of Pennsylvania, takes a holistic approach to learning analytics research, using a variety of methods to study learning and engagement in both online and classroom environments.

Learning analytics, as they improve over time, have the ability to allow future learning platforms to gain a deep understanding of each employee: their skills, strengths, areas for improvement, interests, and more. This type of data, combined with uses of artificial intelligence, can allow the creation of learning experiences that are personalized and truly support the employee. Intelligent use of data in the aggregate form, across all employees, has the potential to provide forward-thinking organizations with the ability to use data to improve learning throughout the organization.

Summary

This chapter explored the technology used to host, deliver, track, and report learning experiences, along with a number of related concepts. Organizations have the opportunity to move away from the limitations of older systems that drive the creation of simple, less-effective learning experiences, to the use of new models and new systems. The world of online learning is changing rapidly, and learning platforms and systems are changing.

CHAPTER 5

Custom Courses and Content

Working With Outside Vendors and Contractors

Nearly every organization, no matter how strong its internal team, has at least the occasional need to bring in an outside company or subcontractor to create an online learning experience or to play a role in the design and development processes.

Common reasons to bring in an outside company or contractor include the following:

- The need to add temporary capacity to your current staff, due to not having enough permanent team members for the work at a particular time;
- The need to limit the time or role of internal team members on certain projects;
- The need to bring in people from the outside who specialize in skills—anything from strategic consulting to, more commonly, specific graphics or animation skills—that that in-house team does not have; and
- An interest in using specific processes, technologies, or software platforms that a particular outside company provides.

It's often helpful for an organization to establish an ongoing relationship with vendor companies, consultants, and subcontractors that it finds to be a good fit. Creating the right partnerships, often so that outside people and teams feel like an extension of an organization's L&D department in many ways, can help tremendously.

Outside companies and contractors can play a variety of roles: it's common for outside e-learning companies to be asked to design and develop online courses, which typically involves hiring a company that puts an entire team on the project. Many organizations also bring in outside assistance for smaller roles—sometimes at a strategic level, but also, and more frequently, at a detailed level; the outside person or team might focus solely on course development, or even a more-specific role such as graphics, video production, animation creation, writing, or editing.

What to Look for in an Outside Vendor or Contractor

As a wise friend of mine says about business dealings in general, the goal isn't to find the right contract, it's to find the right relationship, whether it's with a vendor company or an individual subcontractor. It's always wise to ask to see samples of past work (though sometimes contracts limit what someone is allowed to show) but often just as critical to get to know the people your team will be working with. See if you feel you'd be comfortable in a working relationship with them, whether you're philosophically aligned in terms of both educational/performance philosophy and work processes. Ideally, you want to find people who can work in a consultative way—understand the company culture and audience, create an experience that's what you need. So when it comes to custom work, particularly custom course design and development, my view is that it's best to view this decision like an internal hire—it's not just about what they have produced, but about what they can produce for you and with you. Related to this is one key point to consider when looking at work samples: certainly the graphical look is an important element, but it's sometimes easy to focus on the look at the expense of fully evaluating the effectiveness and relevance of the overall learning experience.

Creating a Request for Proposal (RFP)

The usual process when it comes to soliciting an outside company to create an online course, particularly if an organization does not already have a regular course creation partner company, is to issue a Request for Proposal (RFP). Some RFPs include detailed specifications and are seeking a vendor company to follow them; others are more open-ended and are seeking on outside company that provides value in terms of design and development, starting from the audience's goals and needs and designing a solution that can meet those. My suggestion is that whenever possible, it's better to keep things more open and focused on the goals you would like to achieve more than the specific solutions; very specific RFPs tend to attract responses in which the respondents essentially "color by numbers" based on the provided specification, which generally won't result in the best end product. And the better you understand and can articulate your goals—before even reaching the point of writing an RFP—the better off you'll be in terms of what you want to accomplish and finding people who can help you do so.

RFPs are generally distributed directly to vendor companies of interest, or posted on an organization's website or elsewhere so that anyone can see it and submit a proposal. Nonprofit organizations typically have a few more rules and regulations to follow when posting an RFP than for-profit organizations do. Key things to include in an RFP for the design and development of an online learning course include the following:

- *Background regarding the organization/department:* Even if the RFP is being created by a large, well-known company, it's helpful to provide basic information about the company—for example, even a major retailer would do well to note how many stores it has and in which countries—and the department issuing the RFP.
- *Specifics regarding the project's goals, content (at a high level, at least), and target audience:* I have actually seen a surprisingly high number of RFPs that fail to explain what the goals of the project are, what content it covers, and who it's for. Good learning experience design requires an understanding of the goals, content, and audience, so in order to receive thoughtful proposals, it's critical to explain the goals, content, and audience. It's also very helpful to define what success would look like for this project in terms of the organization's goals—increased sales? Better customer service scores? More efficient employees? The better someone understands the overall goals, the better their design suggestions can be, and the more an organization can benefit from the RFP process and the proposals it generates.

- *Specific roles*: As we discussed earlier, outside vendor companies and contractors can play a variety of roles. If you're looking for people to play specific roles, note that in the RFP. It's also helpful to note the roles that your organization plans to play on the project—this will help set expectations and form the basis for a strong working relationship with whichever company you end up selecting.

- *Specific deliverables*: What end product do you expect at the end of this engagement? A course? A performance support system? Anything that will achieve the goals? Those and more are completely reasonable approaches, and being specific to the degree that you have strong views will help create better proposals and a better working relationship with the team you eventually select. Outside companies won't necessarily be familiar with your culture and norms, so what you think is an obvious end product may not be the way everyone sees it (and someone out there may have great ideas that are worth pursuing!). You may also want to note any expectations regarding additional final deliverables, such as source files of any type. If you have interim deliverables that are critical, such as a prototype version for distribution to an internal audience, those are definitely worth noting; other interim deliverables may be better left to the proposing team to suggest a process, but that really depends on the views of the team writing the RFP.

- *Technical specifications and requirements*: If the learning experience or course needs to be in a certain format, such as SCORM 2004, in order to work with your organization's internal systems, be sure to specify that. Sometimes, there's even a reason to ask an outside company to use a specific authoring tool, such as Storyline, and to provide the Storyline source files at the end of the project so that your organization's team can make changes in-house on their own in the future, or hire someone different to do so. Now, as is typically the case, more requirements tend to limit the creative possibilities, so there are trade-offs in this approach.

- *Project due date*: This one seems simple but can easily be forgotten. It's ideal to include an expected due date, even if the date isn't a hard, unmovable date, so that it's clear to the submitting teams how much time to plan in the project timeline. The timing can also affect the proposed designs and processes—for example, a longer timeline might allow time for more end-user testing.
- *Specific contractual requirements, if any*: Some RFPs are open to contract discussions and terms, some are more rigid in their requirements. If your organization/department has specific requirements, note them in the RFP so that the submitters know what to expect and can proceed accordingly.
- *Timeline for the proposal process*: This typically contains the following dates:
  o The date and time by which prospective submitters should express their intention to submit, so that they stay in the process.
  o The date and time by which prospective submitters can ask questions—typically the process involves people submitting questions and then the RFP team posting a single set of answers to all who expressed interest, so everyone sees all questions and answers.
  o The date and time proposals are due.
  o The potential date range for presentations, assuming you will ask a group of finalists to present. Sometimes this date range is difficult to know in advance, but it's ideal if you can confidently post it.
  o Planned dates/date ranges for notifying recipients, finalizing the contract, and starting the project.

One overall point to keep in mind: when writing dates and times, be sure to be specific about the time zone.

- *A clear process and contact for any questions and for proposal submissions.* Often, organizations ask for any questions to be sent to a particular person or e-mail address, and then all answers are posted on a certain date and distributed to all potential submitters, so that everyone has exactly the same information. Whatever process you use, it's critical to be clear and to put this information in a prominent place in the RFP. The same is true of information regarding proposal submissions; whether you ask for e-mailed documents or for files to be uploaded to a particular online location, it's best to be very clear about the specific process and timing.

- *Specific requirements for the proposal*: It's usual to include at least the following as items that you would like the responders to include in their proposal:
  o Their company background.
  o Bios or resumes of key personnel.
  o A suggested high-level course design—ideally, a course designer would have more time to collect and analyze the content and goals before suggesting an approach, but from a practical standpoint, asking for a design approach at the proposal stage is common and reasonable, and sometimes with screen mockups of early candidate screens.
  o A timeline with interim milestones and review points from the project start through the design and development stages.
  o Samples of past work—submitters often may be limited by previous contracts in what they can provide but should have some samples.
  o References, with their e-mail addresses and phone numbers, who can speak to the submitter's work and what it's like to work with them.
  o A proposed price, or, potentially, alternative prices depending on different options.
- It's also worth noting whether you would like all submitters to follow a particular format in their reply or not (and if so, be very clear about the formatting requirements!). There's a trade-off here: if all proposals are in essentially an identical format, it's easier to compare proposals directly. But enforc-

ing a structure can limit the creativity of the responses or make it difficult for some submitters to clearly communicate their strengths.

Some RFPs include specific course design requirements and look more for development work; there are certainly situations and internal teams for whom this method works well, though my view is that if you're looking only for development work under a lot of constraints, hiring an individual subcontractor may be the way to go. For a "course" or "learning experience" proposal, I typically suggest RFPs that allow for more creativity on the part of the company submitting a proposal. By taking this approach, you open yourself up to new ideas and often better attract the companies and teams who are interested in thinking through complex problems rather than just trying to produce as directed.

Sometimes, RFPs include specific scoring criteria—for example, 30 percent of the score is based on price, 30 percent on the design solution, 20 percent on references, and so on. Often, the need for these criteria is driven by internal processes or requirements; otherwise, it's a matter of the team's preferences.

Another RFP-related issue that is relevant is that of whether to include a budget limit or range in the RFP. Most RFP writers shy away from doing so, generally thinking that if you include a limit or range, all submissions will be near the top of that range. That may well be the case, though it's also true that there are a variety of possible solutions to any learning problem, as we've discussed earlier in this book, and so it is helpful to the submitter to have a sense as to whether a budget might accommodate only a simpler experience or might have room for pricier options such as simulations, virtual reality, high-end video. Some RFP authors try to work around this issue by not specifying a budget number but by asking for proposals to include both "lower-budget" and "higher-end" options; this is often a good approach, particularly if you can also make it clear that you will potentially be open to discussions about pricing. If you can have a price/scope discussion with companies that you are particularly interested in working with, rather than being bound specifically to exactly what is written in an initial proposal, that process can work well. Some organizations, particularly nonprofits, do have reasons why their review processes must be more limited, however.

The RFP Process

We've covered the elements of an RFP itself, but the RFP process involves a number of stages, which we have only begun to touch on. Those stages typically include the following:

- *Writing the RFP*, as covered above.
- *Distributing the RFP*: Different organizations have different processes for this; some, particularly nonprofits, have formal processes and an internal department who handles distribution to companies who have signed up for their system, while others may choose to do some research and reach out to specific companies directly.
- *Reviewing the set of potential submitters* who indicated that they did, in fact, intend to submit a proposal.
- *Accepting questions from potential submitters.* This is typically done by asking all questions to be sent to a specific e-mail address or submitted on a particular website form; then, the internal team at the organization that created the RFP reviews all questions and puts together responses.
- *Responding to questions* (via e-mail or posting/e-mail notification). Typically, all questions and responses are made available to all potential submitters, so that everyone has the same information available to them.
- *Reviewing all proposals, after the deadline for submission.* Whatever your review system is and whether it's formal or informal, it's ideal to have at least a few people with different backgrounds involved in the review, and to take good notes on your thoughts and any open questions you want to ask the submitters.
- *Selecting finalists and conducting interview/presentation sessions.* Most organizations select a handful of "finalists" and ask them to present their proposal, either in person or, more commonly

these days, online in a Zoom or similar meeting. The presentation session provides an opportunity to serve as an interview (for both parties) and to discuss open questions. This is where the open questions from the "review" phase are especially useful.

- *Determining the winner and informing them.* This is a critical step, but in most cases not actually the final step. Some RFPs do include contractual rules or even a contract template, which has the advantage of allowing you to move forward immediately—by the time you select a company, they will have already agreed to the contract terms, perhaps even in a binding format, and finalization is easy. But this process is not always possible, so this stage generally involves reaching out to the winner and beginning a hopefully brief contract process. In some cases, depending on the formality of your processes, you may want to reach out to a potential winner with a concern—for example, you might write something like "we really like your proposal, but is it possible to reduce your price by X amount?"
- *Finalizing the contract.* This depends on your organization; some organizations may want to use their contract format, while others are open to contracts from the company who won the bid.
- *Informing the other candidates.* Timing is a little tricky on this since, ideally, you wait until you have at least a nearly done deal before telling people that they didn't get the job, but on the other hand, it's ethical to not drag out the process unnecessarily or make people wait too long to hear back when they didn't get the work.

Contractual Issues

While contracts should certainly be written and reviewed by your organization's attorneys, it's helpful to be aware of a handful of issues that often come up relating to the particular type of project and relationship that you'd be involved in. Things that often come up include:

- *Ownership*: With a few exceptions, such as those regarding intellectual property (as described below), the organization commissioning the product typically receives full ownership rights to the end product.
- *Marketing and demonstration rights*: Outside vendor companies typically would like to maintain the rights to highlight their work with you, demonstrate it as a past work sample, list it on their website, and even potentially show it at a conference. Different organizations have different rules and restrictions about the limitations on marketing and demos; some organizations restrict demos to specific screens or demo paths, so as not to show too much internal content to the outside world, while others are more open. My view is that if possible, it's better to allow outside companies to show their work with you, and to partner with them regarding conference talks and award submissions.
- *Inclusion of a vendor's logo on a course*: Most internal online learning within an organization is branded with the organization's brand, rather than that of an outside company. But there are certainly times to be flexible, and this issue may arise.
- *Intellectual property (IP) rights*: Sometimes, an outside company uses its existing intellectual property, such as in the form of computer code, to produce a product for you. In those cases, your organization will still want ownership of the end product and rights to do whatever you like with it but carving out an exception to allow a company to retain ownership of its previous IP is common in my experience, and sometimes necessary.

Working With the Company/Contractor That You Select

Once you've chosen a company or contractor to work with—and for the purposes of this discussion, we'll focus on working with an outside company—there are a number of things to keep in mind as you establish and agree on work processes and build a working relationship. The relationship starts with the RFP process and then continues, and ideally strengthens, as you work together. Key areas to be aware of, and plan for, include the following:

- *Roles and responsibilities*: From the RFP creation onward, and even more so as a project begins, you'll want to be clear about what roles your team is playing and what roles the outside company is playing. Outside vendor companies may be accustomed to working in different roles than you expect—for example, my own company, Kaleidoscope Learning, typically is involved in the design of a course from the beginning, but on some projects, we're asked to come in later in the process and we don't really have a role, and don't staff for, high-level design concept work. Anything can work, as long as everyone communicates clearly. Outside vendor companies also may think they're doing less than you might expect. I once consulted to a large retailer who was having trouble in a relationship with a vendor company—the project really wasn't moving along. I met with the full team and asked a lot of questions about roles and responsibilities; when I asked who was writing the content for the course, there was a deafening silence in the room—the retailer had expected that the vendor would do this, as is often the case, working from discussions and materials provided by the retailer that formed the basis for the course content. The vendor expected to be given screen-ready content by the internal team at the retailer. Once this disconnect was resolved, the project proceeded ahead once again.
- *Timeline Dates and Flexibility*: It's almost always the case that while the overall end date for a project is usually established before the project starts, there are a number of interim deliverables for review whose dates can't really accurately be determined until early in the project. Interim deliverables tend to include sample screens, content documents, a prototype version, and other items that mostly will be part of the foundation of a course, an actual element in a course (such as a video), or a version of a course in an in-progress state. It's

often helpful to be open about when there might be flexibility and when there's no flexibility possible. Good e-learning work is creative, and therefore sometimes a little extra time on a deliverable can go a long way. Often, some deliverables have hard, unmovable deadlines—for example, a version of a course for target audience members to test might require a lot of planning and organization to arrange the testers' time, so moving that deadline would be difficult and expensive— but others, such as documents to be evaluated by an internal team, might slip a couple of days without any consequences. In order to maintain an ideal, professional working relationship with an outside company and also make the most of their abilities, it's ideal to be flexible where it makes sense to do so.

- *Subject matter experts and their roles*: Ideally, an e-learning course design and development process begins with a content collection and analysis phase, in which the course designers read materials, watch videos, and have discussions with subject matter experts (SMEs). Under the best processes, the SMEs play a critical role in providing course content at the level of realistic situations, necessary skills, common misconceptions people have, and key information, but then it's up to the course designers to create a learning experience to help their audience learn the skills. Sometimes, SMEs are accustomed to a role in which they provide key points and expect the course designers to essentially create online slides and quiz questions around those points. That's unlikely to be the best learning experience, as discussed earlier, so it's ideal to set the expectations of the SMEs as experts rather than as course designers themselves. It's also advisable to include the SMEs in content review phases to help ensure accuracy, realism, and that the language used will feel right to the target audience.
- *Additional process guidelines*: Each company you work with may have its own specific process, but any sound e-learning design and development process includes the following:

o *Content collection and analysis:* The design team gains a deep understanding of the content, goals, and audience for the course. This typically involves a mix of work, including reading and viewing materials and having discussions with subject matter experts and other stakeholders.

o *High-level experience design:* The design team defines the plan for the learning experience—what type of experience or experiences will be included? A course might be simulation-focused, or a MOOC, or another method, or a mix of methods, and this is the time to define that.

o *Screen design:* What will key screens look like, graphically? The goal here is to define, and agree on, the overall look and feel of the learning experience. While the key focus here is on the learner's experience, this is also a time to make sure you're aware of any branding requirements and design any screens with those in mind.

o *Detailed design and content development*: This includes a variety of work, with specifics depending on the particulars of the course content and design. Typically, this involves detailed activity design and then development work, including writing, video creation, animation creation, and graphics work. Ideally, the vendor process involves client feedback at appropriate key points, and sometimes feedback from end-users and SMEs.

o *Course versions for review and testing*: Most course design processes involve a few versions for review by the client team, again often including end-users and SMEs. It's often useful to have an early demo or prototype version for review and then a beta version before the final release. Some processes involve a pilot test before a wide rollout; the trade-off there is that it takes time and effort to run a good pilot test and make changes, and also delays the release to a wider audience, in exchange for a product that may be improved. Finally, it's critical for a pre-release version, such as a beta version, to be tested on the exact technical platform where it will be deployed. Even a SCORM course running in an LMS may run into a few small technical surprises that need to be addressed before release and finding this out earlier rather than later is key.

Summary

Working with an outside e-learning company can potentially provide an organization with a way to create learning experiences that are difficult or impossible to create in-house, and can be a cost-effective way to add temporary resources. There's a lot to consider when looking to find, hire, and work with an outside vendor company or subcontractor, and a variety of different skills and approaches that outside companies offer. In this chapter, we have covered a number of major things to consider throughout this process.

CHAPTER 6

Maximizing Your Online Learning Strategy

How can you get the most out of online learning within your organization and make a true, lasting impact on organizational learning and culture? Sometimes, it's all too easy for a learning and development (L&D) group to be tasked with numerous projects that are rushed and end up being low-impact and limit the opportunities to re-envision the types of initiatives that the department can produce. In this chapter, we'll discuss a few things that an organization and L&D department can do in order to make the most of online learning.

Team

The specifics of any ideal team's composition vary depending on the organization, but there are a handful of key skills that a team is likely to need in order to be successful at creating online learning experiences that make an impact. Smaller organizations—and some larger ones—can incorporate some of these skills via outside consultants, contractors, or vendor companies, though there are certainly advantages to having a very skilled in-house team. Key skills include:

- *Consulting skills:* These allow a team member to understand a target audience and their needs. This is a critical, and often underrated, skill when it comes to deciding what online learning initiatives to move forward with and what type of experience to create. It's ideal to be skilled at speaking with members of an employee group and asking open-ended questions in order to gain a deep understanding of their workflow, style, and needs.

- *Collaboration skills* enable working with other departments, including subject matter experts, higher-ups (to gain funding approval for projects), and the organization's IT department, among others.

- *User experience design skills:* It's critical for an online learning team to understand how to design products that suit their target audience. A nice definition and description of "user experience" comes from the well-known Nielsen Norman Group (www.nngroup.com/articles/definition-user-experience):

> *"User experience" encompasses all aspects of the end-user's interaction with the company, its services, and its products.*
>
> *The first requirement for an exemplary user experience is to meet the exact needs of the customer, without fuss or bother. Next comes simplicity and elegance that produce products that are a joy to own, a joy to use. True user experience goes far beyond giving customers what they say they want, or providing checklist features. In order to achieve high-quality user experience in a company's offerings, there must be a seamless merging of the services of multiple disciplines, including engineering, marketing, graphical and industrial design, and interface design.*
>
> *It's important to distinguish the total user experience from the user interface (UI), even though the UI is obviously an extremely important part of the design. As an example, consider a website with movie reviews. Even if the UI for finding a film is perfect, the UX will be poor for a user who wants information about a small independent release if the underlying database only contains movies from the major studios.*
>
> *We should also distinguish UX and usability: According to the definition of usability, it is a quality attribute of the UI, covering whether the system is easy to learn, efficient to use, pleasant, and so forth. Again, this is very important, and again total user experience is an even broader concept.*
>
> *While it may not be possible or practical to have a full-fledged user experience (UX) expert on the team, having a team that includes people who have UX skills and experience at some level is definitely advisable.*

- *Online learning design skills:* While this may seem obvious on the surface, online learning design skills aren't necessarily the same skills as those needed to design a classroom course. There's certainly often overlap between the skills of an online learning designer and an instructional designer and also between the skill set of an online learning designer and that of a UX designer. An online learning designer should be familiar with technology and potential creative uses of it, in order to be sure not to simply translate in-person course methodologies.

- *Online learning development skills:* Online learning developers—and people play the role of both designer and developer in many organizations—have technical and media skills that enable them to create courses and elements of courses. These skills typically include experience with off-the-shelf authoring tools such as Articulate Storyline, image editing programs such as Adobe Photoshop, and programs such as Camtasia with video editing features, potentially along with higher-end tools and also software packages that use templates to speed up the creation of media, such as Vyond, an animation program, and Canva, a graphics program.

- *Writing skills:* These are critical—great writing underlies a great learning experience in all sorts of ways; whether the experience centers around stories, video scenarios, or even is more focused on content explanation, writing that's clear and in the appropriate, respectful style for the audience and course design is crucial.

- *Reviewing, editing, and testing skills:* Everyone needs an editor, and in the world of online learning, the notion of "editing" expands to reviewing content in various forms—writing, graphics, video, and other—and to testing courses for potential user experience or technical issues.

There are lots of different ways to account for all of these skills on a team as a whole, but however your team is structured, all of the skills are important to have.

Technology

Along with having the right team, you'll want to have the right technology for your needs. Typically, this involves licenses to the appropriate development software that your team works with—Storyline, Camtasia,

Adobe's Creative Cloud suite (including Photoshop), and other programs. And the learning management system (LMS) and, potentially, learning experience platform that your company uses will play a key role in learners' experiences as well. LMSs tend to not score high when it comes to usability and to learners' views of them. There's also a variety of options out there in terms of different platforms that can host courses, including EdX and Coursera for MOOCs and a number of platforms from different companies that serve different needs.

Culture

Online learning as a field often seems to be perceived as being built around content and access, with a goal that can be described as "let's get this content out there so everyone can get to it." But a content-centered approach tends to be ineffective educationally—people primarily learn facts, rather than becoming involved in a learning experience that helps them perform their roles better—and also doesn't typically create an ideal culture. Online learning is often one of the first experiences that a new employee has, and something that most employees will experience regularly in any organization, large or small. So online learning can be quite influential when it comes to an organization's culture. For example, I designed a video-based customer service training course for Target Stores (described in Schank 1997) a number of years ago. Prior to the rollout of this course, new customer service, or "guest service," employees were trained fairly informally, with an experienced employee giving them a few tips, and also via a training manual from corporate L&D. The new course focused on an interactive simulation in which new employees interacted with customers, who appeared on video with particular, realistic problems, and then the employee needed to decide how to handle the customer and situation. At any point, the employee could ask for advice from a coaching component, and depending on what the employee chose to say or do, the customer might be happy, or might be angry, or anything in between. Additionally, a coaching component, with text and videos of experts, would pop up at opportune moments to give feedback and offer advice.

The customer scenes were well-scripted and the customer characters were memorable and realistic, if occasionally on the dramatic side of realistic. One unexpected effect of the training was that employees would, according to several managers, sometimes discuss the characters from the training with other employees during their breaks—this was considered unusual, and was credited to the realism of the characters and the overall design of the experience. Further, it's likely that employees who took this type of training, which was clearly applicable to their job and also respectful—even as brand new, entry-level employees, people weren't asked to sit in a room and memorize information, and they weren't talked down to—had a positive feeling about the company culture and felt valued and respected. This is just one example, but at all levels, creating useful learning and performance experiences that are meaningful to the target audience has the potential to positively influence an organization's culture.

It's also crucial to create a culture for your own online learning team; one key in my view is to work to structure the roles so that the team works on thoughtful and creative work as much as possible. It's all too easy for a team to fall into simply making small changes to existing products, spending time hassling with the LMS or other internal technology, and manage to become burned out without really getting to do the work that they are passionate about, which is also the work that can have a great impact! The best ways to accomplish this depend on the team and the organization, and can be a challenge, but can include everything from making sure that everyone on the team has the option to work on a variety of different types of projects to working out efficient processes so that the team's time overall can be spent thinking and creating as much as possible.

Summary

As we've seen, it can be easy for an L & D group to spend its time responding to requests and making minor updates rather than re-envisioning what an organization's learning experiences can look like. While some amount of smaller work is always necessary, it's critical to establish an environment, team, technology, and processes that can push the organization forward.

CHAPTER 7

Creating Successful Online Learning

The Research

There has been a movement toward *evidence-based approaches* (Clark 2010) in online learning, and learning designers have, more and more, looked to employ research findings into their work. This is very much a positive development, though one key strategy when it comes to employing research findings is to take advantage of research in a variety of fields, including education and cognitive science, and to integrate the findings into your overall design process. It's surprisingly easy sometimes to lose the forest for the trees if you focus solely on research; the goal is to design a learning experience that will resonate with and help its target audience, and research findings certainly inform that process but are far from the only relevant factor. In this chapter, we'll explore several research areas that are particularly relevant to the design of successful online learning experiences.

Situated Learning

A lot of traditional learning methods, those based around learning facts and passing information-based quizzes and tests, involve learning that's significantly outside of the context in which the information will be used. In organizational learning even more than in schools, the end goals center around skill development and behavior change; there's not a tremendous amount of value to simply knowing information unless it helps you to do something, such as making a decision or performing a task. There's often a gap between learning experiences and the actual work; one of the key contributions of a forward-thinking L&D group is to narrow that gap and tie learning experiences to the jobs and tasks that people will perform.

Situated Learning: The Research

The key foundational theory relating to this area is called *situated learning*—the first core concept is that that "…knowledge is situated, being in part a product of the activity, context, and culture in which it is developed and used" (Brown, Collins, and Duguid 1989). A related concept is that of *authentic activities*, which are defined as "the ordinary practices of the culture" (again from Brown, Collins, and Duguid 1989). The key point of Brown, Collins, and Duguid's seminal work is that knowledge is not separate from doing; therefore, effective teaching and learning methods incorporate context and actions on the part of the learner, and authentic activities are ideal. The concept of situated learning was described extensively by Lave and Wenger (1991) in their own seminal work. Lave and Wenger popularized the idea of *communities of practice* (explored in more detail in Wenger 1998), which emphasizes the social aspects of learning, and Collins and Brown later described the concept of *cognitive apprenticeship*, a way for people to develop cognitive skills. Key elements of the Collins/Brown model (Collins, Brown, and Newman 1989; Collins, Brown, and Holum 1991) were nicely described by e-learning researcher Clark Quinn (2016) as follows:

- Modeling the desired performance
- Coaching performance
- Providing and releasing scaffolding
- Having students articulate their understanding
- Guiding reflection on their understanding
- Encouraging exploration of new problems.

Situated Learning: Putting It Into Practice

These concepts support the types of learning methods we discussed earlier, such as learn-by-doing simulation, and the idea of integrating learning experiences into employees' workflows and creating more just-in-time performance support experiences that help people perform tasks, while not necessarily directly focusing on learning (the goal is for employees to do their jobs better and more easily; learning is in service of that goal). A few key things to do in organizational learning that relate to the situated learning research are as follows:

- *Focus learning experiences on doing rather than on memorization*: People learn best in context, as Collins, Brown, and Duguid explained, and this leads directly to the idea that the best organizational learning experiences generally involve people performing realistic tasks rather than memorizing information. Online simulations, as discussed earlier, provide one method that can work very well and is in alignment with situated learning principles.
- *Make use of just-in-time performance support:* Not all experiences that improve job performance need to be "learning" experiences; the goal is for employees to perform their jobs well, rather than to "learn" in a more abstract sense. Just-in-time performance supports products—experiences that help people perform better, such as a website that telephone- or chat-based customer service agents can use during an actual customer interaction to decide how to respond, as one example—are clearly as situated as can be, helping people perform by providing them support in the context of the actual, real-life task.
- *Consider the employee's workflow* when designing any product intended to improve learning and performance: While performance support products are intended to be part of an employee's workflow, it's also critical to make sure that learning experiences work as well as possible within the work that an employee is doing—this might include structuring learning experiences so that they, or parts of them, can be done in an appropriate amount of time given the employee's job responsibilities; providing a way for employees to find exactly the learning experience they need when they need it; or other things.
- *Ensure that the situations in a learning experience are realistic and are relevant to the employee*: The concept of authentic activities is critical; employees need to feel that their learning is meaning-

ful and relevant to them, and from a performance standpoint, the more often an employee can handle realistic on-the-job situations, the better. One key goal of a well-designed learning experience is to build useful experience for an employee, who can then leverage that experience in the actual job.

Motivation

Motivating people to fully engage in their learning experiences is a critical issue, and one that is often misunderstood. Many traditional learning experiences, in both schools and the workplace, use grades and scores to motivate learners—the thinking is that learners will pay attention and perform at their best in order to achieve a high score. While some people certainly do find good grades and scores helpful in motivating them to learn, stronger approaches typically revolve around creating experiences that are meaningful and relevant to learners and are motivating without the need for external factors.

Motivation: The Research

There's been a fair amount of work in the literature, perhaps most notably by Thomas Malone (1981), on motivation and learning. Motivation can generally be either *extrinsic*—due to outside factors, such as students being motivated to get a good grade or employees motivated to please their supervisor or get a good evaluation—or *intrinsic*, in which the activity itself is inherently motivating and is essentially its own reward. A large percentage of organizational learning experiences rely heavily on extrinsic motivation, such as quiz scores or even leaderboards, in which employees compete for the best performance and see how they're doing. The generally accepted thinking in the motivation-related research is that intrinsic motivation is preferable to extrinsic motivation, and that in learning experiences, building an experience that is intrinsically motivating is key. Many educational games function by taking an inherently boring experience and tacking on a game to it, rather than building in game-like elements, such as challenge, into a realistic experience.

Motivation: Putting It Into Practice

Organizational learning experiences will certainly be more inherently interesting and motivating to people if they are designed in a way that's clearly meaningful and relevant to them. Building experiences around realistic situations that employees will face on the job is a good way to accomplish this. It's also critical for the overall style of the experience to be respectful; traditional e-learning often talks down to people and makes learning feel like a chore. Instead, the goal should be to create experiences that people genuinely are excited about; as one example, a course Kaleidoscope Learning designed for attorneys, covering how to work with pro bono clients, highlighted stories from an experienced attorney about her own experiences—including some difficult ones—as well as video scenarios that followed the interactions between an attorney and his client. This level of realism worked cognitively—people's understanding was grounded in real examples rather than limited to abstract principles—and also motivationally, in that the scenarios and expert attorney were compelling, interesting, and relevant.

Design

What does "design" mean? Often, when people think of the design of a learning experience, they think of graphics, or screen layout. But design in e-learning really refers to the entire experience. There's a wonderful quote from Steve Jobs about design: "In most people's vocabularies, design means veneer. It's interior decorating. It's the fabric of the curtains and the sofa. But to me, nothing could be further from the meaning of design. Design is the fundamental soul of a human-made creation that ends up expressing itself in successive outer layers of the product or service" (Meier 2019). That's a very flowery, Steve Jobsian way to explain design, but in my view, it's accurate: the key to the success of the Target Guest Service video simulation that we discussed earlier is that it was well-designed at many levels, starting with choosing simulation as the way to teach customer service, down to detailed design decisions such as the types of coaching and feedback and the nuances of the customer characters. In learning, design—true design—is everything.

Design: The Research

Usability expert Don Norman wrote a book called *The Design of Everyday Things* back in the late 1980s and then revised in 2002 (Norman 2002), in which he provides and analyzes examples of objects that we interact with and how they are designed, in all aspects—not just visually, but how they are designed to work, and to be used by people. One of Norman's examples is actually of a teapot that looks beautiful but, due to the positioning of the handle, is completely unusable (Norman 2002). Norman's book is fascinating, and also very relevant to online learning design.

Design: Putting It Into Practice

Designing a learning experience starts with gaining an understanding of the goals, audience, and content, and then coming up with a plan for a solution. The ideal solution involving any job performance area might include a mix of re-engineering processes, providing learning experiences, and providing just-in-time performance support.

When designing an online learning experience, a number of factors come into play:

- *The specific goals and audience*: What problem is this experience helping people solve, and who's the specific target audience? The better you understand your goals and audience, the better equipped you are to design an ideal experience for that audience. While each individual person may have different preferences, using general characteristics of the target audience works well here—what's their workday and workflow like? What style of experience might be appropriate? How comfortable is the audience with different types of technology? What type of language should you use (everything from formal vs. informal to specific terms)?
- *The world of potential creative ideas*: What product could you design to meet the needs of this audience in all ways, to produce something that (like any "usable" product) is enjoyable, effective, and satisfying to use?

- *The constraints*: Timeline, budget, software, and even skill constraints can, and will, limit what you can produce. But in my concept of an ideal design process, the designer thinks big to start and then scales back as needed to meet the constraints— this method pushes the boundaries and often results in a better design than working strictly from the constraints up.

Additional Cognitive Science Research

A few other findings from cognitive science are particularly relevant to the design and development of online learning experiences at a detailed level. Those include the following:

- *Cognitive load theory:* This theory, credited primarily to John Sweller (1988), suggests that because our working memory at any given time is limited, learning experiences need to be designed in such a way that they don't overload people.
- *Clark and Mayer's principles of multimedia learning:* Ruth Clark and Richard Mayer (2011) created a set of principles to follow when creating multimedia learning. These principles pertain mainly to multimedia learning presentations and are at a detailed level—for example, one principle focuses on how to minimize on-screen text if there is also a voiceover (and a related principle notes that if there is on-screen text, it should align well with the voiceover for easier processing by the learner).
- *Spaced learning:* Credited to Paul Kelley (see, for example, Kelley and Whatson 2013), this concept involves reinforcing learning over time, in order to minimize forgetting (the work also made significant use of Hermann Ebbinghaus' forgetting curve (see the republication of Ebbinghaus' work 2013).

Additional Cognitive Science Research: Putting It Into Practice

All of the principles above are wise to keep in mind when creating a learning experience, and particularly at the more detailed levels of the design and development process. Becoming an expert at putting these principles into practice generally requires experience, studying examples, and ideally gathering information from people who have used specific learning products, including learning experiences that you yourself have designed. A few key detailed design practices based on these principles are:

- Break things up into smaller pieces where possible and where doing so doesn't compromise the overall experience, in order to avoid overloading people cognitively.
- When designing a complex situation or scene, consider providing some sort of assistance—in the form of coaching or built into the interface itself—to the learner to make it easier for them to process everything.
- Repetition is often helpful, in some form; people won't always get and process everything the first time through.
- In a video with an expert, it often works for the expert to tell a lot of concrete stories and also to specifically avoid listing principle after principle, which can be difficult to process.
- Think about people's workflow as you design any experience.

Summary

There's a tremendous amount of useful research in several different fields, not solely in the education literature, that can inform the design of online learning. In this chapter, we explored several key theories from related fields and covered some ways to put those into practice in organizational learning design.

CHAPTER 8

When Do You Need Help From an Outside Consultant?

Even if you're in an organization with a large and highly skilled learning and development team, there are a number of situations in which it can be particularly useful to bring in an outside consultant, in addition to the cases in which you might want a subcontractor or vendor company, as we covered in Chapter 5. Consultants will ideally bring a perspective or skill that you may not have on your internal team and that will be useful to have in the short term—though a good consulting engagement can, and should, generally bring about results that will help for some time to come.

Determining when you want to bring in an outside consultant depends on a number of factors, including your internal staff, budgets, and timelines, but there are a few areas in which it's very often helpful to have an outside, experienced perspective. We'll cover a few of those areas in this chapter.

Evaluating E-Learning Effectiveness

It's all too easy for a learning and development team to be overwhelmed with creating learning experiences, causing them to lack the time to evaluate their experiences' effectiveness and to learn from those evaluations. Evaluation skills are also often the type of skills that an outside consultant can bring in, at a more significant level than on most internal teams. Also, evaluation can take place at a variety of stages in the design and development of a learning experience; there's certainly often tremendous value in evaluating a complete learning experience in actual, real-life use, but that's not the only potential use of a consultant who can do an evaluation. Here are some key times to consider having someone come in to look at a project and run a study:

- *At the beginning*: There's often an advantage to having an experienced, outside point of view early on in a project, to help ensure that the goals and audience are clear to an outsider. This role would not really be one of evaluation but would help guide the project's direction. Depending on the experience levels of your team members, an outside consultant might be helpful in suggesting high-level design directions, such as the learning methods to consider or even whether there might be an opportunity to use a newer technology such as virtual reality (VR) or augmented reality (AR).

- *At the screen mockups or partial storyboard/demo stage*: When you have some sample screens ready, or possibly have gone a little bit deeper and have a brief demonstration of a part of the learner experience, in images or a brief interactive program, that's a really good time to bring in an experienced outside eye who can also orchestrate feedback from members of the target audience. Your team will likely benefit from the eye of an experienced consultant, and then there's also both an art and a science to conducting user feedback sessions and reviews in a way that surfaces potential concerns in the form of goals rather than proposed solutions from the target audience. This point is critical and often underappreciated: it's ideal to elicit from the target audience members, in as much detail as possible, anything that they think could be better from the perspective of *goals*—for example, that a user wants to be able to find a particular video clip more quickly. This is very different from asking users what they want to see in the design, such as "add a link here to the introductory video," which is a much less effective method. The goal of this type of testing is to surface issues that the design team can address holistically; responding by simply incorporating user suggestions into the design, while well-intentioned, often results in an experience that loses a lot of its effectiveness and appeal.

- *When you have a complete or partially complete learner experience*—a prototype, alpha version or beta version in software terminology, or, in some cases a pilot study. Prototype versions generally have some content and most features; alpha versions are more complete but still have some bugs and minor missing details; beta versions are essentially complete, pending testing and full QA (quality assurance). Any or all of these stages present good opportunities to bring in an outside eye and, especially, to bring in a consultant who can run a substantial usability study, if you have time, with target audience members. A usability study typically puts members of the target audience in front of a product, with specific use-case scenarios, and asks them to use the product. A consultant in the role of creating and running a usability test will be able to observe people using the learning experience and then, if the learner hesitates, seems confused, or does something unexpected, the consultant can jump in and ask some questions of the learner to understand their reasoning. There are other approaches that can work as well. Based on how early you bring in someone to conduct this type of test—depending on time and budget, it's more than reasonable to conduct tests at several stages of the process—you may have time to make changes in response to the findings of the user tests.

- *When a learning experience has been released and is in use.* Typically, once a learning experience has been released, user studies focus on the effectiveness of the experience rather than specifically on usability issues, though usability is still potentially worth examining at this stage and plays a key role in how effective an experience is. Gaining a true understanding of the effectiveness of a learning experience in real use, out in the field, can be complex. It's common for companies to use post-tests to see if the learner has "mastered" the concepts taught and knows the information provided in a course, but those types of evaluations don't necessarily provide a true indicator of how well someone will be able to perform their role after completing a learning experience. Performance-based assessments (Rudner and Boston 1994; Wiggins 1989)—assessments that ask someone to perform a realistic task rather than simply to answer questions—can be much more effective. It's also ideal to study how people perform on the job once a learning product has been released and used—does their performance improve? That said, the effectiveness of a learning experience can be difficult to determine—even if employees do perform better, was the cause of this improvement the new learning experience or some other factor, even another initiative within the company? It can be difficult to isolate the cause, but an experienced consultant can come in and design an evaluation plan that provides helpful information that can guide future changes to an experience and serve as input to the design of future additional learning experiences as well.

Learning Experience Design Guidance

Even if you have a strong and experienced L&D team, there are advantages to bringing in an outside consultant whose expertise is in learning experience design. It's easy for even an experienced team to become locked into certain ways of doing things, and to certain e-learning design methods and styles. The right outside consultant can bring a fresh perspective and maybe even push your team's design thinking in ways that it has not previously gone.

Advice Regarding Technology and Software Tools

Outside consultants can also bring expertise regarding different uses of technologies and software tools. This type of consulting can involve work at the level of when and how to use, for example, virtual reality (VR), or at a more-detailed level, such as recommending a specific authoring tool for course or animation development. There are advantages to bringing in an outside eye every so often to suggest new possibilities to your team.

Strategic Consulting

How can you best employ technology to improve learning and performance within your organization? That's a significant question, and one that can benefit from an outside consultant's perspective and expertise. Learning and development groups today easily can become buried in the mass quantities of e-learning that they are expected to produce and the technical requirements and conventions that are already in place within the organization. An outside consultant can help you create a strategy to most effectively design, deliver, and evaluate e-learning using various technologies.

How to Select a Consultant

The right consultant to bring in depends significantly on your goals and needs, as well as your team and your budget. So, there are a number of factors involved. Overall, there are several qualifications to consider when evaluating a consultant as a potential fit:

- *Past experience*: The old adage says that there's no substitute for experience, and experience is incredibly valuable in a consulting role—you're looking for someone who can provide immediate assistance, often in a short time period, so you'll want someone who has experience in the particular areas in which you need help.
- *Educational background*: People with a variety of backgrounds can work in the area of online learning and related areas; the best fit depends on the role. Ideal consultants have backgrounds in cognitive science (for usability testing or user experience design work), instructional technology, and other related areas.
- *Philosophy*: There are different philosophies regarding educational styles and how to use technology; you'll generally want someone whose philosophy you appreciate—there may be times to look for someone who is aligned with what your organization is already doing, and times to bring in someone with a different view.
- *Work style*: The better you can understand how a consultant will work and interact with you and your team, the better you can determine if the person will be a good fit. You'll want someone who is organized, responsive, and able to take initiative but is also interested in learning your organization's culture and working in a style that suits you, as the client.

To find a consultant, you might want to ask colleagues, including those in other organizations, for people who they've worked with that might be a good fit. Looking at conference websites in the field can be helpful as well—a number of the speakers in many conferences' programs do consulting work, and by seeing a video of someone's talk or at least an abstract, you'll start to get a sense of who they are. Attending networking events and conferences is a great way to get to meet and connect with potential consultants.

Once you have a consultant, or consultants, to consider, the process can be as formal as you'd like. Typically, you'll want to get a sense of their past work, conduct an interview, ask them to speak with others on your team, and then usually to create a proposal regarding the scope and price of the work. As with any consultant, it's best to have a clear contractual agreement.

Summary

Even when you have a very experienced team, outside consultants can be of great value, whether to address a short-term need or to advise you on a continuing basis. Experienced consultants can provide new perspectives, spark creativity, and provide expertise in specialized areas. The right consultant can help in the short term and set you up for success in the long term as well. In this chapter, we explored a variety of ways to work with consultants and how they might fit in to your department.

CHAPTER 9

New and Upcoming Learning Technologies

As new technologies evolve and reach mainstream usage, the field of online learning has the opportunity to evolve as well. New and emerging technologies such as virtual reality (VR), augmented reality (AR), artificial intelligence (AI), and holograms, among others, have the potential to significantly improve the ability of designers and developers to create enjoyable, effective learning experiences that can be used by large-scale audiences. The key in making the most of new technologies in learning is to design experiences that are specifically suited for, and take advantage of, a particular technology, rather than simply mimicking existing learning methods in a new medium.

New technologies provide the opportunity for the creation of new types of experiences. Each technology provides its own new, and often different, capabilities, which can change the types of experiences we have. For example, not all that long ago, televisions simply displayed whatever was being broadcast on each available channel at that point in time. As a television "user," we could change the channel, change the volume, or turn the TV off—nothing else, really, save for some picture-quality adjustments. Today's "smart TVs" offer a different and greater level of control—we can record shows on a DVR to watch later, watch certain shows on demand, and use apps on the TV to watch programming we choose from services such as Netflix and Hulu. We can also pause and rewind live shows, and fast-forward any recorded and on-demand shows. And we can watch clips from TV shows, or entire shows, online as well. All of these capabilities affect the types of experiences we can have as television users—in the earlier days, we were, out of necessity, very passive TV consumers—there were very few actions we could take. But we now can play a much more active role in TV watching, and the programming options have evolved significantly in order to accommodate that—as one example, TV talk shows go out of their way to create short segments that could potentially "go viral" online. Our uses of television (and of TV shows online) has evolved as well—imagine going back in time, even just to the 1990s, and asking someone if they were "binge-watching" anything; that wasn't a concept at the time because it wasn't even a possible experience that someone could choose given the technology of the times.

In the world of consumer technology, GPS systems and online maps such as Google Maps have completely changed the way we experience taking a trip to a new place. Years ago, planning a road trip involved studying maps, planning a route, and perhaps even getting assistance from the American Automobile Association (AAA). Visiting a friend at their new house often required detailed directions. Now, planning a route is unnecessary—to drive anywhere (or to walk anywhere), just enter the address into your car's, or phone's, map system, and follow along as you go. This is possible because of technological advances; map programs are accurate and, most critically, mobile! A perfect map system that required the user to sit in front of a computer, or in a data center, wouldn't be useful for drivers or walkers. Technology advances along several dimensions completely changed the experience that a user has in driving or walking to a new destination.

The same is true, and should be true, in online learning: as we have new technologies, we can design the ideal experiences that take the best advantage of the capabilities and features that a particular technology has. The goal is not to simply take popular existing learning methods and migrate them to a new technology, but to design and create new learning experiences that make use of what each technology has to offer. People don't use Google Maps solely to plan trips beforehand the way they used traditional maps, because Google Maps offer different capabilities that allow different experiences—they're mobile, they can talk and tell you when to turn so you don't have to look down, and so on. If we viewed Google Maps as just an electronic version of a regular map, we would remain stuck in the same limited set of map experiences forever. And the same is true in learning.

Using Technology to Create New Educational Models—and Bring Back Old Ones

Educational research actually never has supported the idea that the read/ watch-and-test model of education that remains dominant today (both in the class and online) is at all the best model. Back in the old, old days, dating back at least to craftsmen in ancient Babylon under the Code of Hammurabi in the 18th century BC (Encyclopedia Britannica 2021), the *apprenticeship* model was the standard way to learn something. Under this model, people learned something, typically a craft such as black-smithing, by working with an expert; the work typically involved starting with small, simple tasks and then gradually taking on more and more complex roles. The expert played the role of a coach, guiding the apprentice and providing feedback, and often forming a strong relationship with the apprentice. This method has quite a number of qualities that make it an excellent way to learn:

- This was a learning-by-doing approach: people would learn by practicing.
- There was a coach—an experienced person in the role of mentor, providing guidance and feedback.
- Apprenticeships weren't just a one-time event (unlike most training); the apprentice often continued to work with, and consult with, the expert.

Then—if it's such a strong model—why did this model essentially become less prevalent over time? As we needed to teach more people, and cover a much wider variety of topics, the apprenticeship model simply wasn't able to scale up—there are too few experts, they don't have sufficient time, and even in the best case, this is a costly model. The classroom model that we still see today, with one teacher and a large number of students, has been necessary and practical because it scales up. But it's far from ideal! And with new technologies, we can create new types of experiences that embody a lot of the wonderful qualities of apprenticeships and other effective learning models but work for large-scale audiences. Simply taking a classroom model and translating it to a computer, whether with a class or as a self-paced course, completely misses the opportunities we have.

Let's take a look at a number of new and emerging technologies and what types of learning experiences they might be best suited for.

Virtual Reality

Virtual reality (VR) systems allow users to feel fully immersed in an experience. The user wears a headset, which surrounds them in three-dimensional images, and controls their experience via a physical controller—like a video game controller—or, in some cases, via hand gestures. VR systems provide a level of full immersion that's far beyond what someone can experience with a computer or mobile device; when you're wearing a VR headset, the entire real world is essentially blocked out, and you're temporarily living in a 360-degree virtual world that you are able to interact with.

For the purposes of creating learning experiences, virtual reality is an excellent fit for learning-by-doing simulations, in which the learner engages in a realistic experience. This method has been very effective in computer-based versions, dating back in the learning and development/corporate training world to the Boston Chicken cashier simulation in 1991 (see Freedman 1994; Guralnick 1996). Employing this method in an immersive virtual environment can be even more engaging and effective. Virtual reality could be used to help learners explore things—for example, if you'll be working in a restaurant and want to explore your potential surroundings in a way that also provides information, such as showing the oven's dials and what they do (Blum 2017). And learning by doing methods in VR can allow the learner to interact with the virtual world—with a coworker, a customer, a piece of equipment, a building, anything you can imagine—all, if designed well, with coaching guidance and feedback. VR has a tremendous amount of potential in the field of learning and development.

Augmented Reality

Augmented reality (AR) involves technology that allows you to see, hear, and interact with something that's in addition to the real world, in comparison to virtual reality, which creates its own world entirely. Perhaps the simplest (but useful!) example of AR is something that viewers of National Football League games have seen on television for years now: the yellow on-screen line that shows where the team on offense needs to reach in order to get a first down. The actual game is the reality; the yellow line is the augmentation. As a more recent, mobile example: newer versions of Google Maps running on a mobile phone pop up relevant information (e.g., suggesting a nearby museum that might be of interest) based on your location (and these recommendations could be based on other factors, such as your personal interests).

AR's best fit in learning and development is to minimize the need for training by creating more products that are used "just in time" when a user needs them, as *performance support*. The Google Maps example above is an example of performance support for people who are walking or driving; imagine, as one case, a mobile app that allowed a service technician to scan an item they were repairing in order to see, on the mobile screen, exactly what parts were needed and with a link to steps and video instructions for repair. Such a system could help a less-experienced technician perform at a level close to that of an experienced one.

Artificial Intelligence

Artificial intelligence (AI) has been around for quite some time; the term "AI" covers a broad set of meanings, from specific intelligent software techniques to the concept of self-aware AI beings that would take over the world. Today's reality is much closer to the former than the latter (fortunately), and for the purposes of learning and development, there's a tremendous amount of potential for AI to have dramatic and positive effects on learning experiences in a number of ways, including sophisticated analytics regarding each learner's performance and interests, and intelligent interactions with learners.

In order to best explore and understand the possible uses of AI in education and L&D, it's helpful to look back on past uses of AI that are relevant to learning experiences. One of the earliest relevant AI accomplishments was Joseph Weizenbaum's 1966 ELIZA (Weizenbaum 1966), a text-based program (since it was created in 1966) that acted as a therapist; the program would ask the user questions and the user would reply. The program simulated a therapy session but did so without any deep built-in knowledge—for example, if the user said "I'm having problems with my mother", ELIZA might ask, "How long have you been having problems with your mother?" The program worked by recognizing significant words in order to understand what to follow up on—it was not trivial for the program to sound natural (it didn't ask "How long have you been having problems with my mother?" which would be a nonsensical reply) and is considered the predecessor to today's chatbots, which clearly can have uses in learning.

The 1970s saw a lot of work in the area of intelligent tutoring systems (e.g., and notably, Carbonell 1970), programs that played an in-depth tutoring role while working with a student. These systems showed promise, especially in more rule-based subject areas such as algebra. Intelligent tutoring systems have continued over the years, but their use to this point has been fairly limited and even in the best case, it has been very labor-intensive to create the rules for such a system. While intelligent tutoring systems have never fully gone mainstream, researchers at Carnegie Mellon University have found recent success by using AI to create intelligent tutoring systems—that is, creating tutoring systems that learn rather than just teach (Spice 2020)—which is a promising development.

Also in the 1970s, *expert systems*, programs that were created to make decisions the way a human expert would, were an area of high interest. These systems were particularly focused on the medical field and were able to make decisions when presented with information about a case by using a large number of pre-programmed rules. Expert systems remained more works in progress than anything else, for the most part, over the years, but the concepts behind them have influenced software development, particularly that of decision aids and other products that are useful in improving employee performance. So, the concepts are still very relevant to today's L&D groups.

Jumping ahead slightly in time, work into the late 1980s and 1990s on AI in education included learn-by-doing simulations with AI techniques used to provide coaching guidance and feedback, merging some of the elements of intelligent tutoring systems with realistic simulated environments. The first known learn-by-doing simulation for corporate training purposes, by all accounts, was part of my own PhD work, and was a cash register simulation-based training program for Boston Chicken (now

Boston Market), the restaurant chain (see Guralnick 1996 and Freedman 1994). This learning experience included several key elements, incorporating concepts that we have discussed in detail earlier in this book:

- A *realistic simulation* of the cash register that Boston Chicken cashiers would use on the job; the cash register contained lots of special keys and using the register efficiently and accurately took some practice.

- *Game-like elements*: Meters on the screen tracked a user's speed and accuracy at any given time, which added a realistic, game-like challenge. The key is the realism: the meters reflected the actual key metrics that indicated successful performance.

- An *intelligent tutoring component* that was always present to answer, in text, content questions learners asked about what to do next ("Now What?"), how to do so, and why something was important; the three core buttons—Now What? How? and Why?—came from work from Roger Schank and a team of faculty and graduate students at our lab at Northwestern University, the Institute for the Learning Sciences (see Jona, Bell, and Birnbaum 1991). The component also intervened on a learner mistake with advice about what to do differently and why.

This simulation with intelligent tutoring demonstrated the potential power of this type of learning, and we're again at a time where creating intelligent learning experiences can have a widespread impact. AI has the potential to greatly impact learning experiences, along the lines of the ways we've seen in this section and also by providing intelligent analyses of data that help assess a learner's strengths and weaknesses and provide prescriptive direction to the employee.

Adaptive Learning

Adaptive learning refers to a learning system that adjusts itself to a learner's needs based on their performance in the system to that point. Adaptive learning systems often are promoted as "AI" systems, though the current adaptive learning systems are on the lower end of the AI continuum at best. Adaptive learning is very much a current trend in online learning and an area of potential growth over the next several years.

Holograms

The world of holograms—three-dimensional, visually realistic, life-size images—seems futuristic, but holograms already exist even if they are not yet inexpensive enough to be mainstream. There is already some traction in the use of holograms to create realistic, simulated training environments. One prominent technology in this area is Fernando Salvetti's e-REAL product (see, for instance, Salvetti, Gardner, and Bertagni 2019; Salvetti, Bertagni, Gardner, and Minehart 2021), which has been used on a number of occasions for medical training and in other fields. In one of the medical simulations, for example (Salvetti, Gardner, and Bertagni 2019), learners practice on a projected, realistic patient. Another example, also from the medical field, is the use of healthcare simulations in classrooms at the University of Central Florida (UCF; see Baily 2021) using a technology called PORTL. While holograms currently require some equipment and also need space to display the projections, the method has a tremendous amount of potential and is already practical in a number of situations.

Internet of Things (IoT)

The Internet of Things (IoT) refers to objects that communicate with each other via the Internet, with the help of sensors and their own microprocessors and software, among other technologies. The number of IoT devices is growing rapidly; you may have a smart TV, or a smart refrigerator, or an Amazon Dash button that automatically reorders a particular item for you. In the world of learning and development, it's easy to imagine realistic simulations using actual IoT objects, or, likely even better, performance support built in to IoT devices—for example, imagine an air conditioner that's able to connect to the Internet to self-diagnose problems and make a technician's job much easier, or one that can connect to other air conditioning units on the same system as part of that diagnosis process. The possibilities for learning and performance improvement experiences are endless!

Other New and Emerging Technologies

A number of other technologies that are new or emerging have the potential to have an impact on the types of learning and performance support experiences that we can create. Those include the following:

- *5G Networks*: Fifth-generation (5G) cellular networks are much faster than the 4G networks that are still predominant at the time of this writing, and 5G networks provide average speeds of 100 MB per second (Qualcomm 2021), with maximum speeds as high as 20 GB per second, along with very low latency (transmission delays). In practical terms, these speeds put mobile networks at least on par with faster home and office networks, and much faster than many networks. These faster mobile connections provide the opportunity for mobile apps to run more reliably and more quickly, without delays, which allows all sorts of possibilities related to learning and development.
- *Foldable screens*: Some learning experiences require a larger screen, and to this point have been limited to use on laptops, desktop computers, and tablets. For example, imagine an immersive, simulated retail store that a learner needs to explore and manage—that's an experience that loses its feel if it's reconfigured for a small phone screen. But as foldable screens finally become available, that limitation changes—it becomes much easier for an employee to have a larger screen with them at all times.
- *Alternative controllers*: We're all accustomed to controlling a computer with a mouse/touchpad and keyboard, and a phone with our fingers. But there are other controllers as well; gesture control from companies such as UltraLeap has been around for some time in various, not-ready-for-prime-time forms, but still has potential. And brain-based controllers,

such as the one from Emotiv, may continue to have difficulty being accepted by users, but also have potential.

A Potential Future Technology-Based Training Experience

What could a future training experience using advanced technologies look like? Here's a short example of something that could be created in the not-so-distant future. In the sequence below, we'll see a new retail employee in a future training world. The employee begins in a training room but could potentially engage in this learning experience anywhere where there was sufficient space and advanced projectors.

This experience includes a number of key elements that are supported by both research and practical experience as ideal characteristics of a good learning experience, as we've seen earlier in this book. Those elements include the following:

Figure 9.1 An employee in a training room, which is used because it has space and projectors

Figure 9.2 The employee clicks a button and is instantly immersed into a projected retail store

Hello!
Can I help you find anything?

Figure 9.3 A customer is shopping; the employee approaches her and asks if he can help her

Figure 9.4 An artificially intelligent coach jumps in with some advice for the employee

Figure 9.5 The conversation between the employee and the customer continues

Figure 9.6 We jump ahead to the end of the interaction, where the employee sees a summary of his performance

- *Experiential learning in a realistic context:* The employee gains realistic, useful experience in this training. He interacts with a customer in a very realistic way, almost in the ways that an experience would feel with a real customer in a real store.
- *Learning by doing:* In a related concept to experiential learning, the employee learns by doing, not by watching, which results in skill transfer to the job. The employee in this experience doesn't just memorize key principles of customer service, he puts them into practice in similar situations, in feel and in content, to those he will face on the job.
- *Coaching guidance:* The AI coach provides personalized guidance to the employee when he needs it. In this way, the employee gains more than he might from a real-life experience, since someone is there to help him; when working with

a real customer in a real store, rarely is it appropriate for an employee to ask the customer to wait while the employee seeks advice about what to do.

- *Feedback:* The AI coach also provides feedback, in several forms; the employee also receives feedback from the customer character's reactions. We could imagine a version of this experience done as a group, in which other trainees could also weigh in. Feedback from a coach and from peers are also generally difficult to obtain just-in-time in a real situation.

- *A realistic, performance-based assessment and evaluation:* The employee's performance is evaluated on realistic measures, the ones that matter on the job, rather than on how well he can pass a test, as is common in traditional learning.

- *Learner control, but the learner is also assisted and advised:* The learner controls a lot of elements of his experience but also has the expertise and direction of the AI coach.

- *An immersive, personalized, experience:* Overall, this is a deep and immersive experience for the learner.

Such an educational experience is effective and also enjoyable for the learner, and respectful—employees in this type of experience feel as if they are valued, respected members of the organization rather than simply new employees who need to be told what to do. The effects of this type of future learning experience on organizational culture is likely to be substantial; the potential of these experiences is immense.

Summary

In this chapter, we explored a number of new and emerging technologies, such as virtual reality (VR), augmented reality (AR), artificial intelligence (AI), and holograms, among others, and how they could be used to improve learning and performance. The key in making the most of new technologies in learning is to design experiences that are specifically suited for, and take advantage of, a particular technology, rather than simply mimicking existing learning methods in a new medium. These technologies and others offer the opportunity for next-generation learning experience designers to reimagine what education and L&D can be.

CHAPTER 10

The Future of Corporate E-Learning

What's next in the world of organizational e-learning? Change is always difficult and takes time; change in learning and development is perhaps even more difficult to effect, particularly given the vast amounts of existing online learning in any company that would eventually need to be restructured or replaced. Yet as technology evolves rapidly and organizations also look for ways to make online learning more efficient and more appreciated by employees, the future of corporate e-learning may well involve more rapid change than we have seen in the past. There are a number of ways in which corporate e-learning may change in the fairly near future, and we'll take a look at them in the next sections.

Less Training, More Just-In-Time Learning

Traditional corporate training has primarily followed the model of traditional education, in which people take courses as their primary form of learning. We're seeing, and expect to continue to see, much more "just-in-time" learning and performance support, meaning learning, information, and assistance that's given at the time someone needs it, while on the job, rather than during a course. This method is more efficient and focuses on the real goals of an employee, which are about performance rather than solely about learning—the learning should be, as much as possible, in the context of the job and tied to the performance goals.

Fewer Monolithic Courses, More Smaller Learning Experiences

A related concept to that of more just-in-time learning is the idea of courses being more modular and usually shorter. This is another trend that, with good reason, looks to continue. There are relatively few content areas within an organization that require large, long, detailed courses along the lines of a university course—for an employee audience, shorter, targeted experiences tend to be the preferred way to go. These experiences fit better into employees' workflows (as do performance support models, even more so), and are easier to revisit if needed.

Blurring the Remaining Distinction Between E-Learning and Learning

Not that long ago, "e-learning" and "learning technology" were specialized areas within a corporate training group, the domain of specialists. Today, and this will only become more true as time goes on, there's really a minimal distinction between online learning and learning overall. In-person classes and discussions certainly have their role, and will continue to do so (even if some are permanently supplanted by live online events), but the overall role of an instructional designer or learning experience designer will need to include the ability to think through and design online experiences as well as in-person experiences.

New Authoring Tools

Today's authoring tools, the software products that allow learning and development professionals to create online learning, are fairly limited in what they can produce, and for a professional to create more-engaging online learning takes time and often some technical expertise. A lot of the effort that currently goes into learning how to use authoring software and to creating and maintaining courses using existing tools optimally could be better spent in thinking about designing the learning experiences themselves, and authoring software should more easily facilitate the creation of better experiences. Also, as virtual reality, augmented reality, and other new technologies become more prevalent, L&D professionals will need tools that can help them create experiences that make use of those technologies. The set of available authoring tools should increase in the years to come.

A Performance Focus Rather Than an Instructional Focus

Many organizations have already recognized that mimicking traditional instructional models from school (which are often far from ideal in schools, though that's a subject for another book) is not an ideal approach in organizational learning. The goal of organizational learning is to help employees perform well—to ensure they have the knowledge and skills they need and are comfortable, confident, and engaged in their work. A focus on performance rather than instruction—involving more just-in-time learning and performance support—is an approach that should continue to grow more widely in its acceptance.

Growth in the Use of Skill-Based Credentials

Educational credentials provide people with a way to verify that they possess a particular skill; the world of credentials has exploded in recent years as credentials are used more and more by organizations to evaluate external job candidates and sometimes to evaluate internal candidates for a position as well. According to Credential Engine, the leading credential marketplace, there were nearly 1 million credentials available as of 2021 (Credential Engine 2021), and that number will continue to grow.

Greater Emphasis on Learning Sciences

In recent years, organizations have begun to pay closer attention to research that comes from *learning sciences*, which is the term for an interdisciplinary field that includes cognitive science, education, and other areas. Interest in a research-based, evidence-based approach to learning design continues to grow within organizations. In my view, it's critical to understand and make use of research findings but also to do so in the context of a holistic approach to creating a learning experience, one that makes sure not to lose sight of ways to create products that people truly connect with and enjoy using.

Content Reuse

Organizations will look to make use of content in more ways—for example, as part of a training experience as well as part of a just-in-time product, or for use by various audiences. One overall goal organizations have is that of efficiency, trying to create new content only when necessary. Doing this can involve reusing content created by the organization and also outside content, from third-party companies and even content found on the Internet. As with any approach, there are ways to efficiently and effectively reuse content and also ways in which an organization can easily provide experiences and information that are too generic for their audiences if they're not careful. Wise content reuse is an art as well as a science.

A Move Away From Traditional LMSs

In my view, the move away from learning management systems (LMSs) as we know them is long overdue, and organizations have been taking steps to make changes. LMSs have not provided great experiences for employees, either in terms of finding a learning experience they want or need or in terms of the types of learning experiences that they easily support. Even their data tracking, which is a relative strength of most LMSs, is limited compared to what it could be. In my experience as a consultant, many organizations find that their end-user groups and their L&D team members are dissatisfied with their LMS. LMS vendors are working to improve and often radically restructure and redesign their products, learning experience platform (LXP) vendors such as Degreed are growing, and it seems likely that despite their entrenched position as legacy software, traditional LMSs will begin to fade away in the future, replaced by more flexible, advanced systems that are more pleasant to use for both end-users and administrators.

Less Formal and Top-Down Content, More Informal and Bottom-Up Content

Another movement, related in many ways to the moves away from traditional training, is that of looking for ways to better leverage and support informal learning and learning-related content that comes from employees rather than solely from L&D or higher-ups. Creating a culture and also a structure for employees to share knowledge and ideas with one another are critical to any forward-thinking organization and will only become more entrenched in the future.

L&D Integration Within Organizations

Learning and development teams have frequently been centralized "training" groups who would be asked to provide training materials for different audiences within an organization. As time goes on, we've seen a continued shift in the role and positioning of L&D teams to become more deeply connected to the subject matter experts and to the audiences that they serve. Ideally, L&D's integration will continue and L&D will become, more and more, part of each group within an organization, with a seat at the table as decisions are made.

A Growing Worldwide Market

While the e-learning market was already growing rapidly, the COVID-19 pandemic has increased the need for online learning even more dramatically, as organizations have seen that employees can thrive while working remotely. One market research report from Global Industry Analysts (2021) has the 2020 overall global e-learning market at an estimated $250.8 billion in 2020 and then jumping to $457.8 billion by 2026. The e-learning markets in China, Japan, Canada, and Germany are expected to grow particularly rapidly, according to this report. Verified Market Research lists the value of the corporate e-learning market alone at $250 billion as of 2020, with a projected value of over $1 trillion by 2028. Any way you look at it, the global market for e-learning is increasing at a rapid rate.

New Technologies, New Experiences

In my view, the greatest achievements of the corporate learning of the future could be in the creation of new types of learning experiences. We're only in the initial stages of the move, and mindset change, from traditional learning that focuses more on information than skills and judgment to modern methods, able to be implemented on a large scale thanks to technological advances. A combination of technology and creativity, layered on a foundation of learning science, can help forward-thinking organizations take their learning to the next level.

Figure 10.1 shows a view of how learning technologies can be redefined.

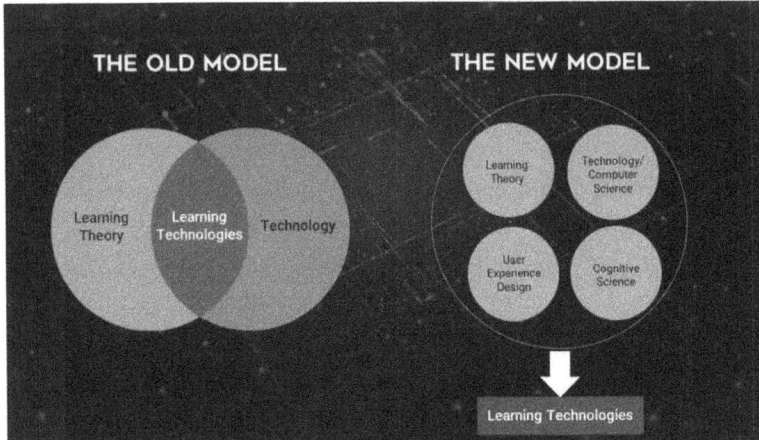

Figure 10.1 Old versus new models of learning technologies

Summary

The e-learning market is growing rapidly, and technological advances allow organizations to roll out inventive, innovative, personalized, enjoyable learning and performance experiences on a large scale. The key in the years to come is for organizations to continue to move away from old-fashioned mindsets when it comes to learning; out will be teaching information, in will be a focus on skills; out will be read/watch-and-test, in will be realistic learning experiences and performance-based assessments; out will be large courses, in will be smaller and just-in-time experiences; out will be one-size-fits-all education, in will be individualized learning and performance plans; and out will be "top-down" learning models that focus only on a teacher, in will be putting learners in control.

As organizations continue to move toward making the above changes, they'll see better and better learning cultures with employees who feel supported and respected by the organization. Particularly as we move to a world in which more jobs are automated and those that remain require thinking and judgment, it will be even more critical for organizations, in order to succeed, to lead when it comes to learning, and especially the uses of technology for learning and performance.

Appendix

For Further Exploration

Industry Organizations

The Learning Guild, www.learningguild.com. Formerly The E-Learning Guild, this group is the best-known U.S. organization for research reports about corporate learning. The Guild produces research reports and runs conferences and webinars. Guild members are substantially from the United States, but the organization has attracted members and conference attendees from around the world.

Association for Talent Development, www.td.org. Formerly the American Society for Training and Development (ASTD), ATD has been around for quite some time and continues to flourish. The organization holds conferences, produces research reports, publishes a monthly magazine and occasional books, and provides certification, among other things. It also has numerous local chapters across the United States, which allow learning and development professionals to connect in person.

International E-Learning Association (IELA), www.ielassoc.org. This international organization covers both corporate learning and higher education, bringing together researchers and practitioners to share ideas and advance the field. The organization holds conferences, publishes academic journals, and runs an international awards program with two major divisions, one for corporate/business submissions and one for higher education.

Industry Conferences and Events

The Learning Ideas Conference, www.learningideasconf.org: Held each June on Columbia University's campus and online, this conference (formerly known as ICELW, The International Conference on E-Learning in the Workplace) focuses on the future of learning—new ideas, new technologies, and how things can change for the better. The conference speakers and attendees are a rich mix of people from corporate learning, higher education, and various research roles from education, cognitive science, computer science, and related fields.

DevLearn, www.learningguild.com/content/24/about-our-conferences: A conference from The Learning Guild, DevLearn focuses on learning technologies. The annual conference includes an expo with vendor booths as well as numerous conference sessions.

Learning Solutions, www.learningguild.com/content/24/about-our-conferences: Another annual conference from The Learning Guild, this conference is intended to provide near-term solutions for e-learning professionals. As with DevLearn, the conference includes an expo with vendor booths as well as numerous conference sessions.

Learning 2021, www.learningguild.com/content/24/about-our-conferences: This annual conference, also from The Learning Guild, focuses on an audience of learning leaders, while the other Learning Guild conferences are aimed more at practitioners.

ATD International Conference & EXPO, atdconference.td.org: An industry standard for years, ATD's flagship event includes a large number of conference sessions plus an expo. ATD also runs a number of smaller national events, and numerous local events via its chapters, over the course of each year.

ATD TechKnowledge, techknowledge.td.org: This ATD event focuses specifically on learning technology and is typically held every winter.

Training Conference & Expo, www.trainingconference.com: Another longtime standard with a large conference plus an expo, run by the group who also publishes the popular *Training* magazine.

Learning Technologies London, www.learningtechnologies.co.uk: Held every winter in London, this conference provides a number of high-quality conference sessions along with a vendor expo, and is generally considered the most popular corporate learning conference in the UK.

Learning Technologies France, www.learningtechnologiesfrance.com: Held every winter in Paris and formerly iLearningForum, this conference also has a large expo along with many high-quality conference sessions. Now a sister conference to Learning Technologies UK, this is generally considered the most popular corporate learning conference in France; many of the sessions at this conference are in French, though the conference also includes a large number of English-language sessions and English-speaking participants.

Financial Services Learning and Talent Development Innovations, www.fintraininginnovations.com/. This conference, typically held twice per year, is specific to the financial services industry. It attracts a very high-end group of L&D professionals in the financial services industry and creates a warm, collaborative environment and an always-interesting and practical program.

Chief Learning Officer Symposium, www.closymposium.com: This well-regarded annual event typically focuses on a smaller set of talks by very experienced, engaging presenters, with more of a strategic than tactical focus.

Online Educa Berlin, oeb.global, is a large, annual European conference and expo that includes both organizational learning and university-based learning. This conference has been a mainstay in Europe for years and attracts people from around the world.

Additional Resources

Brandon Hall Group, www.brandonhall.com. Best known for their comprehensive awards program, they also provide consulting, webinars, research, and more.

Bersin by Deloitte, www2.deloitte.com/lk/en/pages/human-capital/topics/bersin-by-deloitte.html, provides research and advisory services focused specifically on corporate learning.

Chief Learning Officer (CLO) magazine, www.chieflearningofficer.com/, provides articles and events. CLO also runs the annual Chief Learning Officer Elite awards program, which accepts entries from organizations and focuses on awards for organizations with elite learning strategies.

Training magazine, https://trainingmag.com/, provides a monthly magazine in both print and digital format, as well as additional content and courses.

iJAC, www.i-jac.org, the *International Journal of Advanced Corporate Learning*, is an academic journal focusing on work related to corporate learning.

eLearn Magazine, elearnmag.acm.org, published by the Association for Computing Machinery (ACM) includes a variety of articles, many of which focus on corporate learning.

Learning in the Modern Workplace, www.c4lpt.co.uk/blog. This blog contains posts from Jane Hart, founder of the Centre for Learning and Performance Technologies in the UK.

The Art & Science of Learning, www.theartandscienceoflearning.com, is the home for a series of podcasts about learning in the workplace and beyond, hosted by Dr. Kinga Petrovai.

Learnlets, https://blog.learnlets.com, is a blog from Dr. Clark Quinn, a well-known e-learning researcher and speaker who focuses mainly on workplace learning.

References

Association for Talent Development. 2021. "What Is Microlearning?" www.td.org/talent-development-glossary-terms/what-is-microlearning

Baily, L. 2021. "UCF Installs Impressive Dr. Hologram Technology to Improve Healthcare Simulation Education." *Healthy Simulation*. www.healthysimulation.com/33616/ucf-hologram-simulation-technology/

Baron, D. 2019. "Here's Why You Should Be Incorporating User-Generated Content." *ATD Insights*. www.td.org/insights/heres-why-you-should-be-incorporating-user-generated-content

Bersin, J. 2019. "Learning Experience Platform (LXP) Market Grows Up: Now Too Big To Ignore." *Josh Bersin: Insights on Corporate Talent, Learning, and HR Technology*. https://joshbersin.com/2019/03/learning-experience-platform-lxp-market-grows-up-now-too-big-to-ignore/

Blum, P. June 14–16, 2017. *Workplace Learning with eduBeacons*. International Conference on E-Learning in the Workplace. New York.

Bonwell, C.C., and J.A. Eison. 1991. *Active Learning: Creating Excitement in the Classroom*. Washington, DC: George Washington University, ERIC Clearinghouse on Higher Education.

Boris, V. 2017. "What Makes Storytelling So Effective For Learning?" *Harvard Business Publishing—Corporate Learning Blog*. www.harvardbusiness.org/what-makes-storytelling-so-effective-for-learning/

Branscombe, M. 2020. "You've Switched to Microsoft Teams, but Here's Why Yammer Still Matters." *TechRepublic*. www.techrepublic.com/article/youve-switched-to-microsoft-teams-but-heres-why-yammer-still-matters/

Brown, J.S., A. Collins, and P. Duguid. 1989. "Situated Cognition and the Culture of Learning." *Educational Researcher* 18, no 1, pp. 32–42.

Carbonell, J.R. 1970. "AI in CAI: An Artificial-Intelligence approach to Computer-Assisted Instruction." *IEEE Transactions on Man-Machine Systems, MMS-11*, pp. 190–202.

Casebourne, I. 2015. "Spaced Learning: An Approach to Minimize the Forgetting Curve." *ATD Insights*. www.td.org/insights/spaced-learning-an-approach-to-minimize-the-forgetting-curve

Christensen, H. June 10–12, 2009. "From Training to Performance Support: When *Where* and *When* Become *Here* and *Now*." International Conference on E-Learning in the Workplace, New York.

Clark, R.C. 2010. *Evidence-Based Training Methods: A Guide For Training Professionals*. Alexandria, VA: Association for Talent Development.

Clark, R.C., and R. Mayer. 2011. *E-Learning and the Science of Instruction*, 3rd ed. New York, NY: Wiley & Sons.

Collins, A., J.S. Brown, and A. Holum. Winter 1991. "Cognitive Apprenticeship: Making Thinking Visible." *American Educator*15, no. 3.

Collins, A., J.S. Brown, and S.E. Newman. 1989. "Cognitive Apprenticeship: Teaching the Craft of Reading, Writing, and Mathematics." In *Knowing, Learning, and Instruction: Essays in Honor of Robert Glaser*, ed. L.B. Resnick, 453–494. Hillsdale, NJ: Lawrence Erlbaum Associates.

Credential Engine. 2021. "Counting U.S. Postsecondary and Secondary Credentials." https://credentialengine.org/counting-credentials-2021/

Cross, J. May 2004. "What Is Workflow Learning?" *eLearn Magazine*. http://elearnmag.acm.org/archive.cfm?aid=1013188

Dewey, J. 1938. *Experience & Education*. New York, NY: Kappa Delta Pi.

Ebbinghaus, H. October 1885/2013. "Memory: A Contribution to Experimental Psychology." *Annals of Neuroscience* 201e, 20, no. 4, pp. 155–156.

Encyclopedia Brittanica. 2021. "Apprenticeship." www.britannica.com/topic/apprenticeship

Feigenbaum, E.A., and B.G. Buchanan. 1993. "DENDRAL and Meta-DENDRAL: Roots of Knowledge Systems and Expert System Applications." *Artificial Intelligence* 59, nos. (1–2), pp. 233–240.

Freedman, D.H. August 1994. "The Schank Tank." In *Wired* magazine.

Freeman, S., S.L. Eddy, M. McDonough, M.K. Smith, N. Okoroafor, H. Jordt, and M.P. Wenderoth. 2014. "Active Learning Increases Student Performance in Science, Engineering, and Mathematics." *PNAS Proceedings of the National Academy of Sciences of the United States of America* 111, no. 23, pp. 8410–8415.

Gery, G. 2001. "Performance Support—Driving Change." In *The ASTD E-Learning Handbook*, ed. A. Rossett. New York, NY: McGraw-Hill.

Global Industry Analysts. 2021. "Global E-Learning Industry." www.reportlinker.com/p03646043/Global-Mobile-Learning-Industry.html

Greeno, J.G., D.R. Smith, and J.L. Moore. 1993. "Transfer of Situated Learning." In *Transfer on Trial: Intelligence, Cognition, and Instruction*, eds. D.K. Detterman and R.J. Sternberg. Norwood, N.J.: Ablex Publishing.

Guralnick, D. 1996. "An Authoring Tool for Procedural-Task Training." [PhD Dissertations]. Northwestern University's Institute for the Learning Sciences.

Guralnick, D. June 11–13, 2014. *The Role of MOOCs in Corporate Training and Professional Development*. International Conference on E-Learning in the Workplace. New York.

Guralnick, D. 2019. *Learning Experience Design: Concepts*. International Conference on E-Learning in the Workplace, June 10–12, 2020. New York.

Guralnick, D., and J.C. Kinnamon. March 16–18, 2016. *iMOOCs: An Interactive Approach to Large-Scale Collaborative Learning*. Learning Solutions Conference. Orlando, Florida.

Guralnick, D., and J.C. Kinnamon. June 13–15, 2018. *Turning Subject Matter Expertise into an Interactive Learning Experience.* International Conference on E-Learning in the Workplace. New York.

Guralnick, D., and D. Larson. 2008. "The Cultural Impact of E-Learning and Intranets on Corporate Employees." In *Connected Minds, Emerging Cultures*, ed. S. Wheeler. Cape Canaveral, FL: IAP.

Haselton, T. 2021. "Google Maps Has a Wild New Feature that Will Guide You Through Indoor Spaces Like Airports." www.cnbc.com/2021/03/30/google-maps-launches-augmented-reality-directions-for-indoor-spaces.html

Heath, C., and D. Heath. 2010. *Switch: How to Change Things When Change Is Hard.* New York, NY: Crown Business.

Hoekman, R., and J. Spool. 2010. *Web Anatomy: Interaction Design Frameworks that Work* (Voices That Matter). Berkeley, CA: New Riders.

Interaction Design Foundation. 2021. "User Centered Design." www.interaction-design.org/literature/topics/user-centered-design

Jona, M., B. Bell, and L. Birnbaum. 1991. "Button Theory: A Taxonomic Framework for Student-Teacher Interaction in Computer-Based Learning Environments." Technical Report #12. The Institute for the Learning Sciences, Northwestern University, Evanston, IL.

Kelley, P., and T. Whatson. September 05, 2013. *Making Long-Term Memories in Minutes: A Spaced Learning Pattern From Memory Research in Education.* Frontiers in Human Neuroscience.

Kolb, D.A. 1984. *Experiential Learning: Experience as the Source of Learning and Development.* Englewood Cliffs, NJ: Prentice Hall.

Lave, J., and E. Wenger. 1991. *Situated Learning: Legitimate Peripheral Participation* (Learning in Doing: Social, Cognitive and Computational Perspectives). New York, NY: Cambridge University Press.

Malone, T.W. 1981 "Toward a Theory of Intrinsically Motivating Instruction." *Cognitive Science* 4, pp. 333–369.

Marcus, J. September 12, 2013. "All Hail MOOCs! Just Don't Ask if They Actually Work." *Time Magazine.* https://nation.time.com/2013/09/12/all-hail-moocs-just-dont-ask-if-they-actually-work/

McGill University. 2021. "A Brief History of MOOCs." www.mcgill.ca/maut/news-current-affairs/moocs/history

Meier, J.D. 2019. "25 Best Lessons from Steve Jobs." *Medium.com.* https://medium.com/@jdmeier/25-amazing-lessons-from-steve-jobs-the-greatness-distilled-series-760a831d0908

Merl, C. 2009. *Intercultural Communication in the Advertising Industry: How Communities of Practice Enable Organisational Learning and Knowledge Sharing Processes Across Cultures.* Germany: Südwestdeutscher Verlag.

Newell, A., and H.P. Simon. 1972. *Human Problem Solving.* Englewood Cliffs, N.J.: Prentice-Hall.

Nielsen, J. 2000. *Designing Web Usability*. New York, NY: O'Reilly Media.

Norman, D. 2002. *The Design of Everyday Things* (2002 edition). New York, NY: Basic Books.

Pappano, L. November 02, 2012. "The Year of the MOOC." *New York Times*. www.nytimes.com/2012/11/04/education/edlife/massive-open-online-courses-are-multiplying-at-a-rapid-pace.html

Qualcomm. 2021. "Everything You Need to Know About 5G." www.qualcomm.com/5g/what-is-5g

Quinn, C. 2016. "Cognitive Apprenticeship: Develop the Thinking for Outcomes Needed in Today's Workplace." *Learning Solutions Magazine*. https://learningsolutionsmag.com/articles/1987/cognitive-apprenticeship-develop-the-thinking-for-outcomes-needed-in-todays-workplace

Rossett, A., and L. Schafer. 2007. *Job Aids and Performance Support: Moving From Knowledge in the Classroom to Knowledge Everywhere*. San Francisco: John Wiley & Sons.

Rubin, J., and D. Chisnell, D. 2008. *Handbook of Usability Testing: How to Plan, Design, and Conduct Effective Tests*. Indianapolis, IN: Wiley Publishing, Inc.

Rudner, L.M., and C. Boston. 1994. "Performance Assessment." *ERIC Review* 3, no. 1, pp. 2–12.

Ruiz-Primo, M.A., D. Briggs, H. Iverson, R. Talbot, and L.A. Shepard. 2011. "Impact of Undergraduate Science Course Innovations on Learning." *Science* 331, pp. 1269–1270.

Rustici Software. 2000. "What Is SCORM?" https://scorm.com/wp-content/assets/old_articles/whatisscorm/What%20Is%20SCORM.htm

Rustici Software. 2021. "What is the Experience API?" https://xapi.com/overview/

Salvetti, F., B. Bertagni, R. Gardner, and R. Minehart. 2021. "Digital Learning and Medical Simulation." In *Innovations in Learning and Technology for the Workplace and Higher Education Proceedings of 'The Learning Ideas Conference' 2021*, eds. D. Guralnick, M.A. Auer, and A. Poce eds. New York, NY: Springer Nature.

Salvetti, F., R. Gardner, and B. Bertagni. 2019. "Teamwork and Crisis Resource Management for Labor and Delivery Clinicians: Interactive Visualization to Enhance Teamwork, Situational Awareness, Contextual Intelligence and Cognitive Retention in Medical Simulation." In *Proceedings of the 12th Annual International Conference on E-Learning in the Workplace*, ed. D. Guralnick. New York, NY.

Schank, R. 1997. *Virtual Learning: A Revolutionary Approach to Building a Highly Skilled Workforce*. New York, NY: McGraw-Hill.

Schwartz, J. 2017. "Learning to Learn: You, Too, Can Rewire Your Brain." *New York Times*. www.nytimes.com/2017/08/04/education/edlife/learning-how-to-learn-barbara-oakley.html

SCORM.com. 2021. "SCORM Explained 101: An introduction to SCORM." https://scorm.com/scorm-explained/one-minute-scorm-overview/

Shah, D. 2020. "The Second Year of the MOOC: A Review of MOOC Stats and Trends in 2020." www.classcentral.com/report/the-second-year-of-the-mooc/

Singley, M.K., and J. Anderson. 1989. *The Transfer of Cognitive Skill*. Cambridge, MA: Harvard University Press.

SOLAR, Society for Learning Analytics Research. 2021. "What Is Learning Analytics?" www.solaresearch.org/about/what-is-learning-analytics/

Spice, B. 2020. "New AI Enables Teachers to Rapidly Develop Intelligent Tutoring Systems." *Carnegie Mellon News*. www.cmu.edu/news/stories/archives/2020/may/intelligent-tutors.html

Sweller, J. 1988. "Cognitive Load During Problem Solving: Effects on Learning." *Cognitive Science* 12, no. 2, pp. 257–285.

Sweller, J., P. Ayres, and S. Kalyuga. 2011. *Cognitive Load Theory*. New York, NY: Springer.

Torrance, M. 2021. "What Is xAPI?" www.td.org/magazines/what-is-xapi

Vipond, S. 2016. "Research Spotlight: Corporate Learning Management Systems 2016–2018." *Learning Solutions* Magazine. https://learningsolutionsmag.com/articles/1901/research-spotlight-corporate-learning-management-systems-2016--2018

Weizenbaum, J. January 1966. "ELIZA: A Computer Program for the Study of Natural Language Communication between Man and Machine." *Communications of the ACM* 9, no. 1.

Wenger, E. 1998. *Communities of Practice: Learning, Meaning, and Identity*. Cambridge, UK: Cambridge University Press.

Wiggins, G. May 1989. *A True Test: Toward More Authentic and Equitable Assessment. Phi Delta Kappan* 70, p. 9.

About the Author

David Guralnick envisions a new approach to education and workplace learning. His vision integrates progressive learning theory, advanced technology, and creative, entertaining storytelling to create learning experiences that help people learn to think critically, reflect, and make thoughtful decisions. David holds a PhD from Northwestern University, where his work synthesized concepts from the fields of computer science and artificial intelligence, instructional design, and cognitive psychology. Over the past 30 years, he has designed and evaluated a variety of simulation-based training applications, performance support systems, online courses, mobile applications, and authoring tools for corporate, nonprofit, and university audiences.

David is President and CEO of New York-based Kaleidoscope Learning; President of the International E-Learning Association (IELA) and founding chair of the International E-Learning Awards program; an Adjunct Professor at Columbia University; a regular keynote speaker at international conferences; founder and chair of The Learning Ideas Conference (formerly the International Conference on E-Learning in the Workplace (ICELW)); Editor-in-Chief of the *International Journal of Advanced Corporate Learning* (iJAC); and was founding chair of the American Society for Training & Development (ASTD)'s New York E-learning Special Interest Group. His work has been featured in *Wired* magazine, *Training* magazine (as an Editor's Choice), and the *Wall Street Journal*, and he is the recipient of numerous e-learning design awards.

Index

OTHER TITLES IN THE COLLABORATIVE INTELLIGENCE COLLECTION

Jim Spohrer and Haluk Demirkan, Editors

- *Business and Emerging Technologies* by George Baffour
- *Teaching Higher Education to Lead* by Sam Choon-Yin
- *How to Talk to Data Scientists* by Jeremy Elser
- *Leadership in The Digital Age* by Niklas Hageback
- *Cultural Science* by William Sims Bainbridge
- *The Future of Work* by Yassi Moghaddam, Heather Yurko, and Haluk Demirkan
- *Advancing Talent Development* by Philip Gardner and Heather N. Maietta
- *Virtual Local Manufacturing Communities* by William Sims Bainbridge
- *T-Shaped Professionals* by Yassi Moghaddam, Haluk Demirkan, and James Spohrer
- *The Interconnected Individual* by Hunter Hastings and Jeff Saperstein

Concise and Applied Business Books

The Collection listed above is one of 30 business subject collections that Business Expert Press has grown to make BEP a premiere publisher of print and digital books. Our concise and applied books are for...

- Professionals and Practitioners
- Faculty who adopt our books for courses
- Librarians who know that BEP's Digital Libraries are a unique way to offer students ebooks to download, not restricted with any digital rights management
- Executive Training Course Leaders
- Business Seminar Organizers

Business Expert Press books are for anyone who needs to dig deeper on business ideas, goals, and solutions to everyday problems. Whether one print book, one ebook, or buying a digital library of 110 ebooks, we remain the affordable and smart way to be business smart. For more information, please visit www.businessexpertpress.com, or contact sales@businessexpertpress.com.